How to Have Him Begging for More

100 ways to drive your man wild in bed

how to

HAVE HIM
BEGGING *for*
MORE

100 ways to drive your man wild in bed

ANNA MAXTED

Thorsons
An Imprint of HarperCollinsPublishers

Thorsons
An Imprint of HarperCollins*Publishers*
77–85 Fulham Palace Road,
Hammersmith, London W6 8JB

Published by Thorsons in association with Cosmopolitan
magazine and Hearst Communications Inc., 1999.
Cosmopolitan is a trademark of
Hearst Communications, Inc.

3 5 7 9 10 8 6 4

A catalogue record for this book
is available from the British Library

ISBN 0 7225 38421

Printed and bound in Great Britain by
Caledonian International Book Manufacturing Ltd, Glasgow

Contents

SECTION 2 *Doing It Techniques* 59

Thanks to all providers of sauce material – my husband Phil (but of course!), my mother Mary, and my good friends Sasha Slater, Louise Atkinson and Grub Smith. And my sister Leo! Also, thank you to Mandi Norwood.

Introduction

Sex is a glorious, delicious, sumptuous feast. It is simply one of the most fabulous aspects of being alive. When it's really good it turns you weak with happiness, makes your toes tingle, and your lover fall passionately in lust with you – for the first time, or all over again.

But some women don't make the most of it. They nab themselves a gorgeous man. They go to bed with him. They bounce up and down, giggle, and say 'ooh' a few times. As for the gorgeous men – they're often as bad, if not impressively worse. A lot of them get it up, jiggle it about a bit, pop their cork and conk out.

Then, both parties wonder why their horizontal encounter was like a slice of supermarket pizza: pleasant but nothing special – and who the hell wants to be thought of as *pleasant* in bed? A hot water bottle is pleasant in bed. Sensuous women should be sensational in bed! When you do a man the honour of bonking him, he should need a week off work to recover.

But the truth is, no woman has fabulous, passionate, peel-yourself-off-the-ceiling sex just like that. Whether you're Nikki Taylor or Pauline Fowler, if you want to reduce a man to a limp blob of gibbering awe at your sexual majesty – post-coitally, that is – if you want to get from so-so sex to oh! oh! sex without resorting to surgery, you have to know an extravagant sweep of neat techniques.

And this book will tell you exactly what they are and precisely how to do them. I hope you really like him, because you won't be able to shake him off! *How To Have Him Begging For More* will show you:

■ What turns him on – and how to do it without accidentally killing him. Is your man raunchy, shy, romantic, mischievous, conservative? Is he a lazy long-term lover, or an excitable new flame? Each sex technique is assessed for its compatibility with every type of man, so you can build your very own (*very*) blue print of exactly which sexy tricks will have him on his knees.

■ The sexiest traits – enthusiasm, imagination, confidence, humour, lack of wind.

■ The most essential accessories – your whole body, his whole body, polo mints.

■ The correct attitude – sex is, unlike most aspects of adult life, not a chore. It is fun! It is your chance to play! Even better, it is your chance to play dirty. Don't see it as a challenge or a test, see it as a marvellous adventure. Let the fun begin!

Limbering Up Techniques

Fast food can be immensely satisfying, but eat too much of it and you'll feel sluggish and sick. Likewise, a passionate quickie with your man can be sensational – and it will certainly make him smile on his way to work the next day. But habitually neglecting foreplay is like existing on an exclusive diet of burgers and chips. Soon enough, you become fed up of additives and polystyrene and long for an exquisite three course meal at a beautifully laid table, complete with bone china, tapering candles, and silver cutlery.

The point is, your man has probably had more quickies than sex marathons, because a sex marathon, like preparing a fancy meal, requires time and effort – and you have to wait longer to reap the reward. Whereas a quickie, like fast food, provides instant gratification for impatient people. And that's great for a while, but soon enough, the fast-living start to long for something rather more substantial and special.

Which is why – like a Michelin-starred meal – a long, languorous, lustful build-up before the main intercourse will impress him so deeply, he'll dream about you in business meetings, sigh at the memory while he eats his lunch, and call you – if only to hear the sound of your voice.

The Greased Sex Goddess

Great for the sensuous man, the romantic man, the lazy long-term man, the raunchy man.

Special Ingredient
Nice smelling essential oil (not patchouli, it's so dowdy you may as well stop shaving your armpits, such is the impression it gives).

Example Scene
You tell him to undress, and lie, face down, on the bed. No peeking. If you *must*, put towels down to protect your sheets, but putting towels down isn't very rock 'n' roll. Better to buy sheets that are easily washable. Then, take off all your clothes and smother yourself in massage oil. If you don't mind spoiling the surprise, you may permit him to watch this bit, but truly, it's far more sensual to keep him in the dark, until:

Down to Business
Carefully, and gently, press your breasts against the soles of his feet.

NB the tad conservative man might shriek 'Oh God! That feels weird!' Tell him to shut up. Then, inch by inch, slide your sexy slippery self up his body. Wriggle. Slide. Apply more oil if you need to. And string it out!

Snigger Note

At one point, you will inevitably come nose to butt cheeks, which makes the tad conservative man and indeed, the insecure man cringe slightly. So, if you like, provide a reassuring soundtrack. Even if it's merely: 'Mmm, that feels good'. Or, 'Your bottom is *sooo* sexy it's biteable!' Then, continue wending your merry way up his body, until he can contain himself no longer.

Sex Tip

Do make sure the essential oil is diffused. Pure essential oil will make you both come out in a nasty, stingy, itchy rash. Not quite the effect you were hoping for.

Chase Me!

Great for the romantic man, the raunchy man, the mischievous man.

This is a fabulous technique for when you're short of time. Say you want to ravish him in between getting home from work and going to your parents for dinner, but don't have more than ten spare minutes. Your average romantic man doesn't take kindly to being rushed. He needs a good hour to get into the mood – he can't perform just like that, and if he thinks you're trying to force him into a wham bam, he'll turn all sulky and defensive.

So … use the entire day as foreplay. Leave a succession of increasingly suggestive e-mails on his computer. Or – only if he has a private office – a saucy message on his answer machine. Stick a lustful note inside his briefcase. Phone him and whisper sexy somethings. If you can get him thinking sexy thoughts (and apparently men think about sex every nine seconds so it shouldn't be too difficult), he will have a good nine hours to get turned on.

Real Life Sex

Claire, 28: 'I leave for work an hour earlier than my boyfriend – usually he's still sleeping when I go. So if I'm feeling in the mood, I'll stick a sticky-note on the bathroom mirror, reading "Hey Sexy! Meet me in the kitchen, 8.30pm, tonight." Then, we have this game that we are absolutely not allowed to call each other over anything mundane that day. If he calls me at work, it can only be to confirm our "date," and whisper something rude. Anything like "bring home a pint of milk" is forbidden. I get home before him, and he'll call me *as he's approaching the house*, and tell me exactly what he plans to do to me. It's incredibly arousing for both of us – the sex is awesomely good!'

The Sexy Shaver

Great for the mischievous man, the adventurous man, the raunchy man, in fact, nearly all men – except those with a full beard because you'll have fallen asleep before you've finished.

Comment

While shaving his stubble is very sexy (and incidentally saves your chin skin from being rubbed raw during a long smooch), some men are curiously untrusting, and won't let an amorous woman who's had a few drinks anywhere near their neck with a sharp razor.

However, if he does trust you, and then you cut him to shreds, all is not lost. Says one cakhanded woman, 'I have to admit, I was lethal with the razor, and after I finished my boyfriend had about five nicks all over his chin. So I very tenderly licked them clean of blood* – it was almost vampirical, and very sexy....'

Yet, if your lover isn't into bloodsports and won't let you approach his throat with a thin blade, not to worry –

* (emergency remedy only)

the main idea is to shave each other's pubic hair into pretty patterns – a heart shape, for instance. It's fun, easy and, even if neither of you excelled at art, the results tend to look impressive. Also, it means he pays an inordinate amount of attention to your crotch, and once he's got his head down there ... well, anything could happen.

The raunchy man will enter into the spirit of things. That said, you may need to convince the tad conservative man or indeed, the lazy long-term man. Lazy long-term men tend to regard anything more taxing than a walk to the fridge as not worth their while. The tough guy may also be reluctant at first, particularly if he is playing rugby the next day.

Here's how to persuade him:

- Pour him another glass of wine.
- Say, 'You can do mine first!'
- Or 'This is a fantasy of mine' (men love the idea of fulfilling women's fantasies).
- Or 'Of course, I'll focus exclusively on that area ...'

Here's how not to persuade him:

- 'Go on, a flower shape would look lovely.'
- 'Wait till your rugby lot see it! They'll be so jealous!'
- 'My last boyfriend didn't have a problem with it.'
- 'God you're so uptight.'

NB when you have managed to get him by the short and curlies, treat it as foreplay, not as a work of art. Don't start trying to yank out stray hairs with tweezers, or waxing any stragglers because they spoil the aesthetic effect – the male pain threshold is pathetic and you'll never ever see him naked again.

The Non-Furry Sex Kitten

Your pain threshold, whatever it may be, is a lot higher than his. So, before you suggest the sexy shaver to the excitable new flame, you may wish to go for a tactical bikini wax at your beautician. After all, to paraphrase Jennifer Saunders in *Absolutely Fabulous*, most of us don't have bikini lines, we have bikini paragraphs. Admittedly, it's unlikely to make or break the relationship – but for now, our mission is that he thinks you are a luscious bodacious sex kitten – although not as all-over furry. Hirsute is not cute.

Certainly, a year or so down the line, when your man is utterly smitten and nothing, not even your mother on the phone every Sunday before 9am, will tear him away from you, *then* you can relax your deforestation regime. But, for now, let him continue to lust under the sweet little illusion that, unlike other women, your pubic hair has always grown in a neat little v-shape.

Grown Up Hide and Seek

Lack of variety can kill the spark in the most promising relationship. So this warm-up routine keeps the lazy long-term lover on his toes, gets his heart hammering with lustful anticipation – it appeals to the residual caveman in even the newest of lads – and makes sure he doesn't take you for granted. It also revs up the raunchy man, the adventurous man, the excitable new flame, it can appeal to the tad conservative man, and the shy man because it's exciting, and arousing, without being outrageous.

Ideal Scenario
Late at night, lights off, phone off the hook. Make the atmosphere as spooky as possible. If you can stand it, watch a horror film to psyche yourselves up even more. Then, dress in a skimpy outfit that makes you feel vulnerable, make him count to 100, while you hide. When he does find you, it takes a woman with nerves of reinforced steel not to scream, wriggle, and half-heartedly try to escape.

Tried It, Liked It

Natasha, 29, says, 'We got out *Scream* on video, which terrified me. Then, he had the bright idea of using our mobile phones to spook us out even more. Then we turned out the lights, and he rang me, and growled, "I'm coming to get you!" Well, I'm sorry, but I was gibbering with fright. When he finally found me – I was in a cupboard – I screeched so loud he burst out laughing.

'I was so worked up, I was genuinely trying to escape, so he caught me by the wrists and kissed me, hard. Then it started to be wonderful! Our hearts were thumping like crazy. We ended up doing it in the cupboard standing up. It was cramped and I'm sure we looked ridiculous, but it was beautifully erotic.'

Pre-game preparations/optional additives:

- Tidy objects off the floor, unless you want him to tread on a stray fork and injure himself.
- Shut all pets in a room until the game is over (they love to see what's going on but a big fat ginger Tom making a lunge for that pink dangly thing is going to put both your man, and your ginger Tom off sex for good.)
- Agree beforehand not to exchange a single word, even when your man discovers you. Sniggering may be involuntary – and as long as you're laughing together not at each other then snigger away – but if you want to keep the mood spooky up to the, ahem, climax, then maintain that eerie silence.

Dressing up Without Seeming to Try

Great for the mischievous man, the raunchy man, the excitable new flame.

Getting yourself up in full nurse's regalia can be a schlep (unless you're a nurse). And while the raunchy man may think you'd look delectable wearing your old school uniform, he may well be disappointed because real life isn't St Trinian's, it is a brown A-line skirt. And anyway, if you secretly feel like a nitwit, you will not be the uninhibited flingy-about sexual partner of his perverted dreams...

The simplest solution – which is surprisingly effective – is to go for a mere whisker of promise. If he's clamouring for the sexy schoolgirl look, put your hair in high, cutesy-cutesy bunches. If he fancies you as a biker chick, sling on his leather jacket over your laciest bra. There is absolutely no need to go anywhere near a crash helmet, as it will only turn your perfectly coiffed crowning glory into hat hair (puts the flat into unflattering).

Why so coy? The point of all this forced casualness is to avoid looking foolish. Let's not pussyfoot. You want to wow your man to the extent that he becomes addicted. And while a fully-fledged nurse fantasy in action can be an extremely saucy horizontal treat, if he isn't expecting it, you in uniform will look highly incongruous and possibly ridiculous. Which means instead of going weak at the knees, he may – and the lazy long-term man is famed for this – kill himself laughing. The End. So if you *are* planning to go the full Matron, drop ten-ton hints first, or be prepared for:

The Worse Case Scenario

Veronica, 27, says, 'I'd been going out with Simon for two months, and he kept hinting about me dressing up, so I thought I'd surprise him. I rushed to a fancy dress shop in my lunch hour, hired the Matron kit at great expense, beetled home after work, squeezed into this starchy uniform, wasn't convinced but thought 'He said he'd love it, so he'll love it.' Then, Simon finally walked in, regarded me in horrified disbelief ... and a colleague trooped merrily in behind him. 'Er, hello, darling,' he said. 'This is Trev. Trev meet my girlfriend Veronica. She's er ... a matron!'

Best Case Scenario

- Insist he dresses up in full saucy regalia too – now you are equal.
- Hold a theme dinner party (Hollywood is a good one), – now you have the perfect excuse. Sex between Pamela Anderson aka you, and Arnie Schwarzenegger aka your man, will be a natural after-product, providing you aren't feeling queasy after wolfing too much Tiramisu.

How to Have Him Begging for More

- Agent Provocateur excels in sophisticated but sexy lingerie – and their lines often include delights such as a fabulous French maid bra and knicker set – black with white frilly lace trim. So dress up, a little.

Quick One

Great for all men.

Don a long/short blonde/black wig. It will transform your looks and, consequently, your sexual personality. You'll feel liberated – he'll be captivated.

Snakes and Ladders for Sexual Penalties

In a perfect world, you'd play pool for sexual penalties. Trouble is, unless you or your man own a pub or are reasonably rich, you're (metaphorically) stuffed. However, anyone with a tenner to burn can play snakes & ladders – so why not rush out and buy it? The tad conservative man likes this one, as he doesn't actually have to enunciate his desires. The raunchy man and the excitable new flame have a hard spot for this too – because writing things down allows them to exercise their imagination. The lazy long-term man will find it intriguing at first, although you may have to coax him into something more adventurous than 'you give me a back rub while I lie on the bed with my eyes shut' (but hey, it's a start). The romantic man, the mischievous man and the shy man will jump at this, because it's apparently sweet and such fun. What sane man wouldn't?

The game is simple: each time you go down a snake you will have to perform a sexual forfeit, and vice versa. Every time he goes up a ladder you have to perform a sexual forfeit, and vice versa. Before you begin, both compose a list of raunchy things you would like each other to do. Fold up your requests on separate bits of paper, and stick them on separate mugs. Then, when he slides down a snake, he has to dip into your mug of requests and perform whatever dastardly deed he's had the misfortune to pick. The same goes for you.

Recommended drinks to help the evening progress
Between the Sheets cocktail
⅓ brandy
⅓ curaçao
⅓ dry gin
lemon juice and ice
Frankly, after a few of these, he'll love anything you do to him – and you can get artistic with the ice.

Zabaglione
Yolk of three raw eggs
3 tbsp honey
3 tbsp Madeira
1 tbsp cognac
Put all the ingredients in a bowl and whizz up with a mixer until the concoction turns fluffy. It's sexier served hot, so stick in the microwave for a minute – then tell him it's an aphrodisiac. His mind is the real aphrodisiac, and even if he only half-believes you, he won't be able to keep his hands to himself.

The Frenetic Fitness Trick

Great for the excitable new flame, the sensuous man, the raunchy man.

This is like popping in to see your crotchety Great Aunt Hilda because you happened to be in Frinton-on-Sea for an ironic afternoon at the beach. You fancied an old-fashioned British day out sitting on cold shingle in a stiff wind, but dear Great Aunt Hilda thinks you've made the journey purely to eat stale cake and listen to her complain that Radio Four has gone downhill. So what? – everyone's happy.

With the Frenetic Fitness Trick you get to prance around a gym (and please do take this opportunity to join a ludicrously luxurious health club, with steam room, large swimming pool and huge jacuzzi – more of which later). You can inch a little bit nearer to the body beautiful, and, incidentally, rev up your lover until he just about pops. The excitable new flame will be eager to impress you, so no problems there. Possibly, this isn't the easiest technique to poke the lazy long-term man* or the shy man

---

* If your man – lazy long-term or otherwise – is dramatically unfit, skip this idea as he may injure himself

into action – he tends to be stubborn. But it should have a satisfactory effect on the raunchy man who gets a kick out of seeing other men desire you.

Ideal Scenario

You're not doing much one Saturday. You tell him you're going for a swim and a workout at your health club. Would he care to join you? He can manage a circuit, can't he? His male pride will have him grabbing his trendy trainers (hitherto used exclusively for posing in his favourite bar) before you can say 'exercise gets you in the mood for hanky panky because it makes you feel buzzy, good about your body, and remarkably smug'.

Why this plan won't fail:

■ He sees you in your flashiest, most figure-flattering gym gear.
■ You're inevitably five times as fit as he is.
■ You sweat and men find sweatiness – in this particular scenario – sexy.
■ When you take to the running machine you can't help but jiggle a little.
■ Exercise gets the testosterone coursing through his veins.
■ He will notice that chisel-jawed, hard bodied males are casting lustful looks in your direction, and will therefore have what American psychologists David Buss and Todd Shackleford call a Mate Retention Response. This makes you instantly irresistible because your price on

the open market is even higher than he thought. So, like a cat spraying in the lounge when next door's moggie wanders in through the cat flap, your man will want to make his mark in order to reinforce his belief that you are his property (let him dream).

■ You will be relaxed, flexible, exhilarated and primed for action. This is a good time to try an adventurous position.

The Fully-Clothed Grope

Great for all men.

Here is one of the most irritating conversations a man can have with his woman: 'Talking of sex, my ex used to climax if I rubbed the crotch of her jeans' – What? Yes she was wearing them at the time.' Argh! This kind of indiscretion can take weeks to recover from.

Any reasonable woman could be excused for reacting badly. How dare this vengeful ghost be so easy to conquer, making you, her successor, look like the female equivalent of Ben Nevis but twice as frosty. However – after a short period of bitterness, slamming doors, and recounting the tale to sympathetic friends – you will learn three useful facts:

- Men are fiercely attracted to women who make them feel like sex gods (wouldn't you know it).
- Being skin-on-skin with someone you lust is a superlative feeling. But occasionally caressing them through their clothes makes the fire burn higher.
- Some women can fake it good (*see The Real Cardinal Sin: Faking Orgasms in Section 3 to feel better immediately*).

Pre-Technique Preparation

Unless you are as sensitive as a Volvo car alarm, wear trousers made of light material. No skirts allowed – anything that he can push aside to gain access to skin is cheating.

Step 1

You are driving along the M25 together, or you are sitting next to your man, at a formal meal of some kind – perhaps with prim friends, or family – making polite chat with a table of fellow guests. The most important ingredient is a heavy tablecloth. If you're sitting around a glass-topped table, forget it.

Step 2

There should be no question of you escaping round the back/stopping for a quickie, so rule it out in your head.

Step 3

While keeping up a coherent conversation, allow your hand to creep to his groin or thereabouts. Gently fondle. If he pushes your hand away, insist. He'll get used to it. Pull his hand towards a meaningful spot.

Step 4

If you trust yourself and are daring enough, work some saucy innuendo into the conversation. He will be busting out of his trousers but alas, will have to contain himself until later. Look forward to that 'later'.

Step 5
If he truly cannot wait, retire to your host's bathroom and go for it.

The Low-Fat Frolic

Boy, this is a tedious long-term one, although it does make sense. Feel free to ignore it though as some things, such as a monster bar of Toblerone, can often feel more urgent than sex. Nevertheless, what you eat is what you feel like, so if he survives on English breakfasts and ham rolls, he is going to feel as frisky as a dead pig.

If, however, you can wean him onto a healthier diet (do this sneakily and surreptitiously or the excitable new flame will go right off you), his chances of having a superlative orgasm are far higher. This is because the lower your level of body fat, the higher your levels of DHEA (a hormone that enhances sex drive). At the same time, if his arteries aren't gunked up with cholesterol, the blood flow to his penis will be far heartier.

He barely has to know that he's eating low-fat fare (although you can be a little more blunt with the lazy long-term man), and the only thing he should become aware of is that his orgasms with you are becoming so powerful he feels dizzy.

Some smart ways to get him to eat healthily:

- Bring him a continental breakfast in bed: real coffee (one cup of caffeine can boost the mood), crusty brown bread (white if he's a hard case), honey, real butter, pure orange juice – feed each other. The romantic man and the raunchy man will love this. Not to mention the lazy long-term man, whose goal in life is to do absolutely nothing for himself.

- Later on in the day, if he is a takeaway fiend, steer him towards the least fatty option, i.e. chicken tikka, hamburger (no cheese), thin-crust pizza (preferably non-meat), pasta on a tomato-based sauce, beef fillet. Suggest you both order, then share – so, if he does order the lamb korma (coconut, cream, nuts, heart attack) he only has half a portion.

- Don't keep temptation in the house. Men don't seem to crave types of sugary food in the way women do, yet if he happens across a Mars Bar, his gut reaction is to eat it.

- Alcohol – hmm. Beer has no redeeming qualities. It is, quite simply, your love rival. Best thing you can do is to offer him wine, or a spirit-based drink that will last longer, e.g. Jack Daniels and Diet Coke (tacky, but tasty).

Day of Trash

Let's not call it pornography. Let's call it erotica. Depending on your taste, gather together a host of saucy material. Snuggle up in a sensuous setting, and read out choice scenes from rude books to each other. And look at sexy images. Any man who is worth nabbing, loves and is excited by a woman with a hearty attitude to sex. And frankly, the more that turns you on – pictures of naked men, pictures of naked women, graphic sex stories, whatever – the better.

This technique is fabulous for the lazy long-term man (we're sitting down, remember). Lazy long-term men sometimes need to be reminded that you are in fact, a passionate, hot-blooded sexy woman rather than, say, the person who asks him to put the seat down, reminds him to send his mother a birthday card, and shouts at him for leaving his pants on the bedroom floor rather than in the laundry basket. This technique will surprise and thrill him.

The excitable new flame and the raunchy man just won't believe their luck. The romantic man, the tad conservative man and the shy man might be a little taken aback. Some of these men nurture an old-fashioned idea of women as ladies, with all the ghastly prejudices this entails. You may have to haul him into the modern world via shock treatment. But not too shocking or he may scarper. Start off with some erotic verse, rather than five copies of Razzle.

Hot Tip

If you want your sex life to be everything it can be, it is advisable to start as you mean to continue. Your lover will form an idea of your sexual personality as liberated, wild, fun – and will therefore be more open to and accepting of all your wonderful suggestions. Whereas if you act conservative in the bedroom for five years, you (don't worry about him for the moment) may feel self-conscious about reinventing yourself. (He'll be as chuffed as a chuff of smoke chuffed out of a chuffing train).

Where to start?

- Porn magazines: *Playboy* (it's all downhill from there).
- Erotic books: *Black Lace*, the *Mills & Boon Temptation* range.
- Movies: *The Piano, Wild Orchid, The Cook, The Thief, His Wife and Her Lover, Emmanuelle, Nine and a Half Weeks.*
- Poetry: *Erotic Verse*, edited by Christopher Hurford, published by Robinson.

The Cuddly Toy Massacre

Applies to all men

Lose the cuddly toys. Stick them at the top of your cupboard (on a nice comfy blanket if it makes you feel better), but do not leave them clogging up your bed. Fluffy and Wabbit are as sexy as keeping stale Gorgonzola under your pillow. You won't have him begging for more if his todger is being ogled by an outsize Tigger and a pert Pooh. No man – oh, except the romantic man but even he'll grow out of it – likes stuffed teddy bears, pink or otherwise, especially if they have names, hog the bed, and 'talk.' As far as he's concerned, you lose one sex appeal point per animal. He'll suspect you shop at Laura Ashley and dot your 'i's with little hearts. He'll get the urge to kick and punch Fluffy and Wabbit when you're in the bathroom plaiting your hair. Please, if you want to drive him wild, rather than away, ditch the kitsch.

NB in my life I have met only one man who likes cuddly toys. And he's happily married, so you won't need to impress him.

Construct Your Own Fantasy

This is a game, and thank heaven, it's a helluva lot more fun than Monopoly. Furthermore, you won't end up storming out in a huff because he's trying to bankrupt you. It appeals to all men – although the romantic man and the shy man may need steering away from Enid Blyton towards Jackie Collins.

Either he or you pick a scene that appeals to him and write it down on a big sheet of paper (you may have seen a similar game in *Men Behaving Badly*, where it all went shockingly wrong because Martin Clunes' character introduced an Alsatian into the equation). So, establish your limits before you begin. If you don't want to introduce anything more *outré* than strawberry massage oil, make this plain before he commits his filthy thoughts to paper).

How To Play

1 You write down two scene-setting sentences, e.g. 'I am sitting in a low-lit bar. I am wearing a slinky dress, possibly Versace, but my La Perla knickers were giving me a VPL so they are now in my bag.'

2 Then, you pass the piece of paper to your man. He has to write the next two sentences, e.g. 'I walk into the bar. I see a beautiful woman wearing a jaw-dropping dress, and I cannot take my eyes off her.'

3 Back to you, e.g. 'I notice a man, looking at me. I look him slowly up and down, and wonder if he might come over.'

This is fun, suspenseful and – proving technology does have a function apart from making us want to kick it – superb when played via e-mail. You can adopt any persona you wish but keep a few elements of truth there – so if he has beautiful blue eyes, weave that fact into your text.

(Hint: If he is 5ft 2 tall, don't write down that the dream man is 6ft). You'll commit your most outrageous impulses to paper – and probably end up doing it on the lounge floor. However! For the true sexual adventuress, nothing less than acting out the fantasy (adapting it according to the law and your finances – Whistles rather than Versace?) will do.

Take Him Away from all This

Recipe

■ Devote Friday lunch hour to hunting down a pretty B&B/hotel or sweet-talk a friend/relation with a country cottage. It doesn't have to be extortion to be sexy.

■ Break it to your man that chicken jalfrezi eaten in front of *Die Hard III* is not going to be on tonight's programme.

■ Rush home, pack a toothbrush and clean underwear.

■ Skedaddle.

Unless you have limitless funds, this fast route to great sex can't be over-used. But it's superb for emergencies — especially if the lazy long-term man is bogged down and beleaguered by work, the raunchy man and the sensuous man are getting itchy from dull routine, the romantic man and the shy man need a spontaneity injection, and the tad conservative man* is in need of a different bed to get his juices

---

* Most men will rate you for your spontaneity — of course they want a weekend away, they're just too bone idle to arrange it — but the tad conservative man might get huffy if he's already arranged a game of tennis for Sunday. In which case say we can play tonsil tennis all weekend.

flowing, or if the excitable new flame deserves a reward for services rendered.

Sex away from home is often wonderful because when you pack a bag, get in the car and put your foot down, you shed your worries with every mile. Some might call this 'running away.' Nonsense. Think of it as a modest elope-ment. The lack of distractions, the excitement of scarper-ing, the thrill of being far away from a kitchen sink piled ceiling-high with dirty plates will fill him (and you) with a *joie de vivre*. You'll both want to express it by ripping off your clothes and leaping upon each other.

Real Life Sex

Suzanne, 25: 'Me and my boyfriend always have our best sex away from home. We went to Paris one weekend and the weather was terrible – it pelted with rain. But we had a room with a view, and late at night, we stripped and danced naked on the balcony. It was so exhilarating – the sex was exquisite. Another time we stayed at this cheap family-run B&B in Dorset – it was so relaxing, it was like staying at your auntie's house. We felt naughty but raunchy. There were no distractions. So much sexier than at boring old home!'

The Full Body Caress One

The point is, you're making a fuss. All men — (possibly the shy man may have to be forced) — will love this.

What you'll need:

- One man, freshly bathed.
- A bed or — if possible — a table, plumped with towels to make it soft (you're less likely to get backache if you're not bending over).
- Curtains, as it's better if the room is dimly lit.
- Candles, scented if you like — although some of them stink.

What to do:

- Make sure your fingernails aren't scratchy.
- Make sure the room is warm.
- Have a tape on, with soothing mood music (no Metallica).
- Have a bottle of massage oil ready — warm the bottle under the hot tap, so it doesn't make him squeak on contact.
- Make him lie on the bed, naked, on his back. Encourage him to breathe slowly and deeply, in time with you.

The Actual Massage

The main object is to connect. So always maintain physical contact. Pour a generous blob of oil onto his skin, and start smoothing your hands over his body in long gliding strokes. No wimpiness – use your upper body weight to make the movements firm and deep. Start with the outer reaches of his body: legs, feet, hands, fingers, arms, then move towards the centre – chest, stomach, roll him over onto his back, then onto his front again.

Getting Saucy

As you massage his stomach and thighs, gently brush his genitals. You can draw the tease out for as long as you wish (usually until your arms get tired). When you decide the time is ripe to concentrate on his penis, tantalize him with a variety of strokes:

- Full Monty – cup his testicles in your hands. Then, with the heel of your palm, glide up and down the underside of his penis – make use of its full length.
- Top 'n' Tail – grasp his penis in one hand and bring it down, from the tip of his penis, to its root. When you get there, let go. As you let go, your other hand should be grasping the top of his penis, and sliding down. Maintain the alternate motions, never releasing contact.
- Ecstatic Touch – grasp his penis in one hand and feel its warmth. Hold still for about 15 seconds. Then briskly,

stroke it up and down. Then hold still for 15 seconds again. Then stroke, varying your pace.

At this point, should you wish, you may introduce yourself into the proceedings – although be ready to do all the work. He may be so aroused he'll be desperate to make love to you – alternately, he may be so relaxed, the most he'll be fit for is to lie prone while you bump and grind on top of him.

The Full Body Caress Two

Managing his orgasm is an art in itself. You can either let him spurt at will – he'll thank you for it, because it will be superb at this point, whatever. Or you can attempt to delay and control it – and when it actually happens he'll be so rapturous he'll temporarily lose his power of speech. Here's how:

Suggest he gives you a signal when he's nearing orgasm – the phrase 'Oh. My. God.' might be appropriate. When he gives the signal, slow down the speed of your stroke (he must give you the signal in good time, or else he'll end up coming anyway but with less force because you've just backed off).

Your aim here is to draw out the build-up to his orgasm until he can bear it no longer. Another way of slowing down his orgasm is every time he nears his peak, gently hold the top of his scrotum, squeeze and softly pull down, holding it there for a short while. This will work him up into an absolute frenzy.

Tip to Heighten the Tension
Enhance the sensual nature of this technique by using every sense available to you:

- Let him watch you.
- Murmur sexy words of encouragement to him.
- Never stop touching him, not even for half a second.
- Before he comes, he will release a little pre-ejaculatory fluid. Lick it off (the only time you use your mouth for this particular technique) and kiss him — so that he tastes himself on your lips.

NB the raunchy man and the excitable new flame may actually burst at this point, and the romantic man may find this incredibly sexy. However, if you suspect he is a shy man or a tad conservative he may find this a bit much (the hypocrisy is so great, don't even bother taunting yourself with it).

Put him out of his misery: you'll be able to tell when he can't stand it any longer. So keep stroking fast and firm — and don't stand back (see the perfect end to any blow/hand job).

Wearing Down His Defences

Find some excuse to bend down. A hint of cleavage, a glimpse of bra – any time, anywhere – (preferably lacy and clean rather than humdrum and grey), will awaken his libido if it is napping. Works best with the excitable new flame, but the lazy long-term man is so used to seeing you wander around in your saggy sweatpants wearing a white Jolene moustache, any nod towards sensuality, no matter how small, is gratefully received.

Then what? A saucy thought e.g. 'My. Woman. Breasts. Me. Touch' may cross his mind, but be beaten back by other considerations, e.g. 'But. Tired. Want. Watch. Game'. Fight back. Help him to focus on that saucy thought – or sauce in general. Even if you just say casually, 'I dreamed that we went to your boss for dinner and you touched me up under the table' and leave the room, you force him to picture that scene, however briefly.

If he has any sex drive whatsoever, he may amuse himself by recalling it throughout the day. Let him stew. And when, later, you tickle him at the small of his back in the way that makes him go goosepimply, or go sit on his lap, facing him and nuzzle up, it won't take you long to wear down his defences.

The Principle of Competition

Great for the excitable new flame, the sensuous man, the raunchy man, the tad conservative man.

Men, like women, are turned on by winning. Except, they tend to make more of a chest-beating fuss about it. Winning is important, but in this particular instance, so is playing the game. Challenge him to anything – a game of tennis, an egg and spoon race, an arm wrestle, a Cadbury's Crème Egg eating competition if you must. A friendly (but steely-willed) battle is exceptionally sexy, especially if there is some physical contact involved.

It's best to choose something which will introduce some adrenaline into the equation. So forget golf. Decide whether you are happy to lose, because if you arm wrestle, unless he's the feeblest wibbler on the planet, he's likely to win. Allowing him this silly little victory somehow makes him feel all Tarzan-like, and will make him want to hoick you over his shoulder and cart you off to the bedroom to celebrate his win. (Swallow your pride at this point – you're reaping your reward in other, infinitely more subtle ways).

Real Life Sex

Cornelia, 31: 'My boyfriend and I often have a competition to turn each other on, but it's more emotional than physical. It's mischievous and also a little risky – I wouldn't advise it unless your relationship is rock-solid. But here's what we do – we'll go to a party, and each of us will flirt with other people. Nothing too outrageous – the most I've done is pass a strawberry, mouth-to-mouth, to another guy in front of my boyfriend. The most he's done is have a slow, hip-grinding dance with another woman while I watch. We make it quite plain that we're together, and once other people have established that neither of us are going to physically attack our rivals, they seem to get quite a thrill out of flirting back. We usually have to leave early because we're so turned on.'

Quick One

Simple, but an atmosphere sensation. Go one up on the usual candlelit bonk – tidy your bedroom, buy three packs of night lights – you can get them in bulk, cheaply, from any good candle shop. Go out with your man, have fun, come back. Then plonk him in the lounge and tell him to rendezvous in bed in ten minutes. Arrange your candles all around the bedroom, and light them. Undress in your fairy tale grotto, arrange yourself artistically on the covers, and wait.

The romantic man may think he's died and gone to heaven. The raunchy man could do it in a pigsty and enjoy it – indeed, he frequently has sex in his own bedroom – but most men are suckers for a bit of sparkle. Even the lazy long-term/shy/tad conservative man can't grumble – this is a beautiful, romantic gesture. And, in the nicest possible way, it's meaningless, so even the nerviest man can't accuse you of wanting to marry him (unless you're already married, in which case, Mazeltov).

The Incriminating Letter

Steel yourself, and write him the rudest letter you can muster. Describe exactly what you'd like to do to him. The raunchy man and the mischievous man will have trouble containing himself. The tad conservative man and the romantic man may choke on their toast and marmalade – but a gulp of water will sort that out. The lazy long-term man will at first think he's opened someone else's mail. He'll also get over it.

The excitable new flame is more of a risk – if you want to take it, fine, but as many a Tory MP has discovered, it's unwise to commit your raunchiest thoughts to paper to someone you only know in the carnal sense.

If he's a safe bet, however, detail your fantasies (as long as they involve him rather than some other guy) in purple prose. Maybe dab on a whiff of your perfume, but nothing too heavy-handed (the words should communicate the message pretty conclusively). Then post it.* If you're not articulate at voicing your desires, this is a sexy, effective way of letting him know what you really really want. He can re-read the sauciest morsels, dream about putting them into action, and by the time he sees you – he'll be ready to rock.

* If you don't trust his secretary and/or his flatmates, send it registered post.

Silent Tryst

Great for the excitable new flame, the raunchy man, the shy man (may take some forcing though) and the sensuous man.

Angela, 28: 'The sexiest thing I do is to arrange a silent tryst with my boyfriend. We do it every couple of months – not too often so it remains a real treat – but you need to have a house or flat to yourself. I come home, bath, powder and perfume until I feel like a sensual piece of Turkish delight, crawl into bed, turn off all the lights, and lie quivering in anticipation. The deal is, my boyfriend has a key, and he can turn up at any time between nine and ten p.m. He sneaks in, creeps into the bedroom, and without saying a word or turning on a light, pulls off my knickers, and we have quite rough sex – hair pulling, digging in of nails, the lot. We're both so hyped, the actual sex lasts about ten minutes. Then, without a word, he dresses, and leaves.'

Nude Sketching

It worked for Leonardo DiCaprio and Kate Winslet in *Titanic*. It worked for Gwyneth Paltrow and Ethan Hawke in *Great Expectations*. Why shouldn't it work for you? There is no need to spend vast sums on easels, canvases, expensive oil paints and horsehair brushes – although if you want to buy some of the paraphernalia, it does turn your life modelling class into more of an occasion.

That said, there is no need for either him or you to be good at art, and if you have a tight budget, buy a sketch pad and some crayons – grand total cost: a fiver – then settle yourself seductively down on a comfortable sofa, and request a full-length portrait.

This is a delightful technique, as it forces him to concentrate on the contours of your body. 'Sit' for at least an hour while he sketches you, in different poses, clothed, semi-clothed, or naked. Make the surroundings as atmospheric as possible. Ensure the room has good lighting and that there are as few distractions as possible: no telephone ringing, no television, radio, or music on in the background. You don't have to talk. Just relax and listen to the gentle scratchy sound of his sketching.

The romantic man and the sensuous man will love this idea, as will the tad conservative man. You may be hard pushed to get the lazy long-term man interested in this technique – at first. Explain that you'd like a little something to frame in the bathroom, and he'd be doing you a real favour. Oh go on. It'll only take fifteen minutes. He used to be so creative, it was one of the things that attracted you in the first place. He'll get into it.

The excitable new flame and the raunchy man may be a little impatient as neither usually has to wait this long before you pounce on each other – but this will teach them patience and that waiting for something you really want makes having it all the more sweet.

Cute Note
However ghastly his offering – and prepare to be horrified – say you love it, frame it, and display it in your bedroom/bathroom or – if it's really really frightening – the guest toilet. He'll be touched.

How to Have Him Begging for More

Show Time

Today's project is to touch yourself up in front of an admiring audience of one, then ask him to join in. Those of you who do this with your partner as a matter of inter-course may snort – but apparently, less than 40% of young women indulge in masturbation. A great shame, because if you don't know exactly how to get yourself hot, you'll be ill-equipped to show him how to do it, and sex will be that little bit less wonderful for both of you.

This is, theoretically, a technique for your pleasure, but – unless he is a selfish, juvenile oaf, in which case you should be reading *100 Ways to Make a Man Go* – he will start dribbling at the offer. If he hasn't already suggested it him-self. This technique is beguiling to a man because it fuels a favourite male fantasy: to watch – then join in. The excitable new flame, the sensuous man and the raunchy man will be especially awed. But frankly, the vast majority of men will love it – the ones who don't are no doubt still dealing with some tedious childhood 'issue' and are best avoided.

If you're not sure how to stage your show, think Sharon Stone in *Basic Instinct*. Sit yourself on a chair, across the room from him, dim the lights, let him realize you are wearing no knickers – and let your fingers wander. You may wish to practise in private first so you don't crease up laughing. Maybe choose a soundtrack? Definitely warn him that you're about to put on a sexy treat – and choose your moment. i.e. – not in the middle of 'Match of the Day'.

If you are one of the 60% who don't masturbate, make this one a personal project. Use mirrors, diagrams, cucumbers – whatever it takes to make you familiar with your bits. Then issue your exclusive invitation. Please don't be coy – men dream about this sort of event. He will be desperate to touch. So, when he looks as if he might pass out with lust, let him (touch, not pass out). If he knows what he's doing, encourage him. If he doesn't, put your hand on his and guide him to exactly where you want it.

Hot Tips
Lick his fingers – make sure he's washed his hands first – then place them on a meaningful spot, but allow him to explore every area. Let him discover your personal hotspots. If his touch is too firm or too gentle, too fast or too slow, whisper 'harder' or 'softer' – try not to bark out orders like a navy officer. If you want to make this technique as intimate as possible, sit in front of him, your back resting on his chest, your legs apart, his legs apart.

Quick One

Once he's proficient, suggest a game.

Great for the sensuous man, the raunchy man and the lazy long-term man (he'll get into it), the tad conservative man (it's about time he realised that liberals have more fun), the excitable new flame, and the romantic man (he's got to get the hearts, flowers, flowing hair into perspective).

The Rules
You masturbate each other, the first (or last, just choose which is most likely to make you the winner) one to orgasm must:

- pay the winner a fiver
- take the winner to dinner
- do a naked handstand against the wall and stay upside-down for a minute.

This should appeal to your man's sense of fun (as well as his ego – they can't resist a challenge). You must of course cheat, by saying ridiculously sexy things, e.g. 'mmm, imagine me, you and ...' (insert – if you can bear it – the name of his favourite female celebrity here) '... in a threesome. I'd be sucking your ... and she'd be ...' (insert depraved imaginings here while moaning and describing the sensations you feel). As well as allowing you to win, this underhand strategy lets you shake loose a little or a lot. (You may, of course, use implements on each other – feather dusters, root vegetables, it's up to you).

How to Have Him Begging for More

Do Me a Favour Darling

Introducing the Vibrator into Masturbation
Great for all men.

Men have a dilemma regarding vibrators. On the one hand, they think they're a great, raunchy sex tool. On the other hand, they think they are a replacement penis. Hmm. Yes and sort of yes. So, when introducing vibrators into any sextravaganza, bear this in mind and if for some reason your man is feeling decidedly droopy, it's best not to jump up exclaiming 'I know! Let's use my buzzing friend Mr Willy instead – he never gets tired!'

Saucy Scenarios
Raquel, 28: 'My boyfriend loves to watch me use a vibrator on myself. There's no great flair involved. My most workable position is to kneel down on the floor, facing the bed, pull down my knickers, steady myself with one hand on the bedspread, and gently rub my clitoris with the vibrator's tip. As I near orgasm, I push it in a little, but not much. If I'm feeling horny I can come in about three minutes. But, for drama's sake, I try to make it last longer. My

boyfriend likes to sit behind me, so he gets the rear view. If he faces me, I'll act up a bit, and pull extravagant expressions. Most times, he cannot contain himself – he has to join in. No self-control.'

And then:

■ Ask him to use the vibrator on you – he'll probably get a bigger kick than you will.

■ Use the vibrator on him – buzz it around the base of his penis up and down around his testicles. **NB** the tad conservative man and the shy man might be wary. Reassure him that you aren't going to surprise him with anything untoward.

■ The vibrator doesn't have to be an 'instead of'. He and you can use it to stimulate each other during penetration – try using it to stimulate your clitoris (or wherever) when you're on top, or doing it doggy style.

Sex and Shopping

Great for all men (except lazy long-term if you have a joint account).

Even if this theory didn't work — and it does — it would be included as a matter of principle.

The Theory One
The goodwill generated between a couple when she trots off for an extravagant day of clothes shopping, while he poodles off to play five-a-side football is enough to get both thinking juicy lustful thoughts about the other.

She's delighted she doesn't have to stand in a muddy, freezing field for what seems like three hours, he's overjoyed that he doesn't have to traipse behind her like a lost puppy while she nips just quickly into yet another clothes shop.

The Theory Two
Shopping induces a semi-orgasmic state in most women — flushed cheeks, quickened pulse, a feeling of reckless happiness — and most men pick up on this. Enthusiasm (even if generated by forking out large wodges of cash) is very attractive.

The Theory Three

You are obliged to model your new wares. This involves him sitting on the bed while you pop victoriously out of the bathroom encased in your new slinky kit and parade yourself shamelessly up and down in front of him. You have a valid excuse to sashay and pout and if your retail marathon doesn't lead directly to some horizontal wrestling, you are fully entitled to demand your money back.

Quick One

Great for lazy long-term, shy man, raunchy man (he'll present it to you at your parents' house), excitable new flame.

Send him a card. Inside enclose five tokens, each stating something like 'this entitles the bearer to one blow job on the dining room table' or 'this entitles the bearer to one quickie, in the hallway' or 'this entitles the bearer to one bonk in the backseat of a car'. Be prepared to honour the token whenever he presents it to you. Pray he doesn't present them to you all at once.

Doing It Techniques

A friend, Jayne, grumbled recently, 'It's hard to come up with new ideas about sex. I mean, he just puts it in and wiggles it.' Another friend, Julie, described it as 'glamorized friction'. My, how cynical we are! This section aims to make the putting in and wiggling as glamorous as friction can be! Let's hope your boyfriend used to date Jayne or Julie – he'll seize upon any effort you make like a starving dog offered a chocolate-covered bone. He'll be begging for more, tongue hanging out, panting with pleasure, on all fours.

The Push-Back

The push-back is for the woman who likes what she likes when she likes it.

Great for the excitable new flame, the raunchy man, the sensuous man, the romantic man.

Special Ingredient
A narrow corridor.

Example scenes
Excitable New Flame
You have just returned home after a highly flirtatious date, are consumed with desire, and can barely wait to tear each other's clothes off. You slam the front door, sink to the floor, clamped to each other like, er, people kissing extremely hard.

Lazy Long-term Man
He's spent the last two hours slumped on the sofa, flicking from ITV to BBC1 to Channel Four to ITV, while you slump next to him, eating crisps. You are inexplicably overcome with lust. You rip the remote from his sticky

hand, exclaim 'We're having sex! Now!' and lead him forcibly from the lounge. Pull him to the corridor floor.

Ten Minutes Later

You're on top of him and – as fabulously free-spirited as it is to make fast, furious love on the carpet – it's a tad difficult to get a proper grip. Each time you push down hard, you erode yet another layer of knee skin. But if you don't dig into the carpet, you end up meeting his thrust with a weak bump and no grind.

To put more heft into your hump, spread your legs wider, until your left foot is pressed against the left corridor wall, and your right foot against the right corridor wall. Use each wall to help you increase the strength and power of your pushes.

If, however, your corridor is too wide and/or your legs are too short, no problem. Grab his arms, and raise them above his head, flat on the carpet – as if he was about to dive into a pool. Then, hold onto his arms each time you thrust to increase the pressure.

Wonderful for the man who likes it hard and deep.

Not so good if you haven't had sex in a while, as it isn't exactly the most gentle technique.

When You Do It On The Corridor Floor, make sure:

- All pets are safely shut in another room (nothing spoils a romantic moment like your dog sniffing your man's bottom, or indeed, enthusiastically licking his own a foot away from the hot action).

- The carpet is reasonably clean (why is it called shag pile?) It's uncomfortable enough without the additional irritation of getting crumbs in tender places.

- Your flatmate is definitely out until very late and is not going to suddenly barge through the front door with three friends.

- You have condoms in a coat pocket in the hall cupboard so you don't have to run naked up to your bedroom for a panicked rummage while he deflates downstairs.

- You change positions often enough to prevent your knees from actually starting to drip blood.

Bedroom Technology One

There is little that is quite as stomach churning as lying in your bed, alone, trying to get through *Portrait of the Artist as a Young Man* and being unable to hear yourself read because your neighbour/flatmate/parents are having noisy rampant sex next door. However, the moans, groans, squeaks, squeals, and squelches that are so teeth-grindingly cringeable when emanating from other people, suddenly take on delightfully arousing properties when they come from you and your beloved.

Yet, when you're on the job – while you might be vaguely aware that you're screeching at the top of your voice and he's yodelling like an Austrian goatherd – you tend to be so wrapped up in each other that your sexy sound effects don't register as much as they might, especially if Whitney Houston is blaring in the background. As soulful and mood-enhancing as Whitney is, she is encroaching. Remove her from your stereo, and replace her with a blank tape.

Next time you engage in some horizontal wrestling – tape it. It's probably a good idea to tell him what you're doing – lest he discovers it and assumes you're planning to play it on your next girls' night in. He may also act up to it (some men are unnervingly silent during lovemaking – this may encourage them to vocalize their feelings).

Then, the next time you are about to have sex (with the same guy, that is) stick your personalized soundtrack into that stereo – and make love to it. The raunchy man, the sensuous man and the romantic man will go for this in a big way. The lazy long-term man may need some arm-twisting, but will get into the swing of things. If the tad conservative man protests too violently, give in gracefully. A shame, because the raunch value of your own sounds of passion echoing around the room courtesy of Sony surround sound knocks spots off Whitney – and it's the perfect choice if you don't feel up to seeing your own bottom on television in glorious technicolour.*

What to say to convince him:

- Afterwards you can destroy the tape.
- I don't think you realize how sexy you sound during sex.
- My 'ex' was too square to even try it.
- I'd like to listen to it on my Walkman on the train journey to work.
- Only thing is, do I have a tape that lasts 90 minutes?

---

* If you do feel up to it, see Bedroom Technology Two.

What not to say to convince him:

- I could play it next time your parents came round, haha!
- I will not leave it lying about, not after last time's fiasco.
- Oh but I love listening to that funny snuffly-snort sound you do.
- It's imperative that I have a taped record for my collection.
- Why, do you think I might blackmail you with it one day?

Bedroom Technology Two

Part one was for shy retiring types. Part two is for people who like to show off. Men tend to love it even more than the tape recorder ploy, as they can direct should they wish (and they usually do). Now, the video camera is known for its capacity to kink up an encounter (as if the nation splashed out for the sole reason of wanting to appear on *You've Been Framed*) but it has lost its novelty value. The Polaroid is usually purchased for illicit reasons, and it's fun but limited. The latest toy is the digital video camera. Expensive, flashy, impressive.

The digital video's possibilities as a sex tool are endlessly rich. To be brutally honest, there's little difference between a normal video camera and a digital one – except that you can download your saucy images onto your computer. The point however is, it is an exciting, state of the art gadget – and most men (apart from, perhaps, the romantic man who prefers things to be quaint) cannot resist a new gadget. He can fidget with smart technology, play the voyeur, watch television, and indulge his passion for you simultaneously. He'll be so excited, he'll want you to start posing for him straight away.

Real Life Sex

Helen, 25: 'I loved the digital camera. It brought out the performer in me! I was prancing up and down the hall in my knickers, pouting for the camera, fancying myself rotten. My boyfriend loved it because he rarely sees that side of me. I much preferred it to taking Polaroids – everything has to stop while you wait for them to develop! With this, he took about 15 snaps – I could tell he enjoyed playing the role of leering director! Then we cosied up and peered through the viewfinder, deleted the pics we didn't like, then downloaded the snaps onto the television. It was exhilarating and sexy – we left the rudest image on the telly and continued from there. Now we're saving up for a digital video!'

Making A Mess

Great for the excitable new flame, the raunchy man, the mischievous man, the sensuous man, the shy man (it will bring him out of himself, so to speak) the romantic man.

One of the most tedious things in life is tidying up, which is why anyone who can afford it, gets a cleaner. One of the most natural things in life, however, is making a huge mess. Making a mess is enjoyable, naughty, and – in the right circumstances – arousing. So, avail yourself of a huge (old) King-sized sheet/waterproof groundsheet/plastic sheet from a supermarket, push all your furniture out of harm's way – even cover the walls in plastic sheeting if you think they're at risk (hint: they probably are).

Once you have that lot, choose your personal ingredients – anything edible, spreadable, and great for wallowing in. Then strip off, dive in, and make like a pair of hippos in mud.

Suggested ingredients	Amount	Pros	Cons	Tip
Chocolate gateaux	seven	luxurious, delicious	costly	perfect for a birthday sex surprise.
Baked beans	twelve tins	cheap, hilarious	you'll reek of tomato sauce	don't eat too many or you'll blow him away (in the worst possible sense).
Cream	four spray cans	the squirting competition	may lead to anarchy	cool in the fridge first for that extra frisson (then lick off).
Honey and Sugar Puffs	approximately four jars and two 750g boxes	smearing yourselves in honey, hugging then rolling in the sugar puffs is a truly surreal experience	you may die laughing before you actually do it	best if you have a sweet tooth.

All men (and women, let's face it) are kids at heart, and being naughty and making an outrageous, disgusting mess, and rolling about in it is a pleasure we forgo when we leave school. The excitable new flame will delight in this idea, (although he may suggest it's at your place as will the raunchy man). The lazy long-term man, surprisingly, will show enthusiasm (he likes the idea that he can eat during) and the romantic man will eagerly agree (as long as you suggest a glamorous food to roll in). The tad conservative man will come round to it – all you have to say is 'but darling, the principle is really no different from rugby'.

Coming Together

Ah yes. The perfectionist's sex technique. Coming simultaneously imbues you with a fabulous afterglow of
togetherness. It has an excitement value which can only
be compared to an (exceptionally good) game of snap. It
makes you feel as if you are in harmony. All of which are
great reasons to attempt it – although when you don't
come together, there are compensations: you both experience two orgasms. Never mind – this technique will
enable you to enjoy one, superlative orgasm (and you can
always do it again).

The good news is, it takes practice. But you both have
to learn control. His method of control probably amounts
to thinking about Jabba the Hut eating spinach.

- First (and you can both practise alone before trying this
  together), start to arouse yourself until you feel you're
  about halfway to orgasm. Then, by breathing slowly and
  deeply (rather than thinking gross thoughts) try to lower that level, without climaxing.
- Second, bring your arousal level to simmering-point,
  and stay there without boiling over, so to speak. Do this

by breathing deeply again, and reducing the stimulation slightly. Be aware of what will make you boil over.

■ Now (and this is now, after a few weeks of practice) you are equipped with the ability to hang on while your partner catches up with you in the arousal stakes, and vice versa. Rather than say 'ready steady go!' or indeed, 'snap!' agree on a signal – it might just be 'oh yes!' – then do whatever it is that actually pops the cork.

This technique will not be necessary for the lazy long-term lover because, no doubt, you are so in tune you can come together any time you choose. Anyhow, depending on your man, you may wish to keep this technique a secret. Often, the excitable new flame comes first because he's so darn excitable, so he may think you're criticising unless you make this request carefully. The raunchy man will love the result, but not the homework. The romantic man might think it should just happen. If you suspect any of these to be the case, and are willing to do all the work, then practise alone and – gee, one night it *will* just happen.

The Great Prostate Fiddle

Some men are in ecstasy when you touch this area – some men are five feet across the room if your littlest finger so much as wanders butt-wards. This is when you find out if your raunchy man is really, secretly, a tad conservative. It is when you discover how to arouse your excitable new flame into a roaring bonfire or, indeed, reduce him to a damp squib.

If you haven't ever discussed the matter with your lazy long-term man don't assume he loathes the idea – he may be too shy to tell you. After all, the sexual ego is such a vulnerable thing, to enunciate the phrase 'Babe, I'd love it if you poked your finger up my anus' is a risk. For all he knows, you'll think he's ridiculous, weird, or disgusting, and will run away laughing, leaving his dignity drooping.

You shouldn't though. There are highly sensitive nerve-endings in his prostate gland, located a few inches up his bottom – and if you gently push your finger in until you feel a little bump, then stroke it softly, he may go absolutely wild. You will get a strong indication of how wild he will go if you caress around his butthole with your finger first. Make the move slowly enough that he is aware of your intention and has the option of leaping away before being impaled.

Unless your trips to the video shop are that much more adventurous than most people's, you will be doing this in a raunchy context. If he likes having his prostate tickled – this gland is the male equivalent of the G-spot – you can use the technique to bring him to erection, or orgasm, enhance a blow job, intensify the pleasure of intercourse. And gardening or museum visits, come to that, but it's probably best to restrict the practice to a private, romantic setting.

Four finger tips:

- Make sure your nails aren't jaggedy.
- A lubricant, like Vaseline, will ensure smooth passage (terrible pun intended).
- He should have the courtesy to make sure the area is clean, if you get my drift. If not, you are entitled to withdraw the favour (and finger) until he improves his bottom-wiping technique.
- This is a germy area, so – in the least offensive way – you may want to wash your hands before touching your vagina/mouth/his mouth etc. afterwards.

Giving his Penis the Treat of its Life

Oh My God Oral Sex!
If you want to be a swot, buy a dildo to practise on. That is, if you don't already own one. Just don't ever practise before locking the door to your bedroom, and ensuring your opposite-door neighbour isn't peering, agog, through her window.

   Directions:

- Abandon all sense of modesty.
- Don't just pounce on his penis. Work up to it slowly, kissing, licking, blowing, teasing. Make him beg.
- Using your tongue – and your imagination – begin to explore his penis. Start at the head. Swirl your tongue around it, use quick flicking movements, and slower, languorous ones as if you were tasting an ice cream in a cone.
- Use your hand to grip the base of his penis firmly – it will stop him thrusting and give you a degree of control – as you tease and flirt your way down the shaft and up again. Take your time, use firmer tongue strokes.
- Then, close your lips snugly around the head of his

How to Have Him Begging for More

penis, so about one centimetre of it is in your mouth. Your teeth should be nowhere in sight.

- Slide your mouth up and down his penis, sucking fairly vigorously, maintaining a firm mouth-hold, and taking it in as far as it can go. To give yourself a break, swirl your tongue around the head.

- Try to establish a rhythm and aim to relax your throat muscles. (Use the dildo to practise on – as it's unflattering to a man if you retch when his penis is in your mouth. More importantly, it's highly unpleasant for you).

- Rather than merely bobbing up and down, vary the treatment by moving your head in a circular motion.

- Use your saliva to maintain lubrication.

- Pay special attention to where the head of his penis meets the shaft on the side away from his belly – the star point. If he isn't circumcised, it's where the foreskin is attached. It is an exquisitely sensitive spot, and if you gently flick or tap your tongue tip on it, be prepared for the consequences.

Extra Flashy Blow Job Techniques

Once you can perform a perfectly wonderful blow job, you may want to start adding the odd frill and thrill. The idea is to wow him and then — just when he thinks he cannot possibly be wowed any further — raise the stakes. But don't rush to introduce the extras, otherwise you'll spoil him.

Use of Temperature: Cold

Have a glass of iced water by the bed, then, when he's not expecting it, pop an ice cube in your mouth and flick it and your tongue around the head, and the star point. Extra strong mints,* ice cream, or – if you're desperate – mouthwash will also do the trick (useful if you want to hurry along proceedings).

---

* Start off with a Polo mint rather than the nuclear strength kind – better a pleasant tingle than a casualty case.

Use of Temperature: Heat

Take a swig of warm tea/coffee/herbal concoction before bearing down on him – the warm liquid sloshing around the head of his penis along with your tongue will make him shiver. Not too hot though or you'll have some explaining to do in casualty.

Bubbles

Another remarkable sensation is fizziness. You can use Coca Cola, or sparkling mineral water if you're a health freak, but the classiest, sexiest drink is still Champagne. Cool in the fridge first for a double whammy. (It, not you).

Gooeyness

Nutella chocolate hazelnut spread is far more delicious than chocolate body paint. And its consistency is gooier than more expensive chocolate sauces. Nutella, we may therefore conclude, is the most advisable chocolate choice for fellatio. The only danger is that your attention is diverted and you go off and make yourself a sandwich. But, assuming you have staying power, spoon the sauce out of its jar and drizzle it prettily onto his penis. Then enjoy your semi-edible dessert.

NB even when his penis isn't chocolate-covered, when you perform a blow job, pretend it is – it boosts your enthusiasm.

How to Have Him Begging for More

Madness

This irresistible tip first appeared in UK Cosmopolitan, in a fabulous article written by the excellent journalist Lisa Sussman. In it she quoted a woman who – with laudable originality – used to fry onion rings and toss them onto her boyfriend's penis (maybe practise on the dildo first so he doesn't wilt while you retrieve onion rings from the lampshade), then munch them off. Sex is fun, remember?

The Exquisite Hand Job

Depending on your level of determination, you might practise strengthening your arm muscles by – I kid you not – doing press-ups. Most women have poor upper body strength, and if your triceps and biceps are as weak as diluted water, after approximately four seconds of masturbating him your arm will feel as if it's about to fall off, your rhythm will go haywire, and he'll have to take over while you nurse your arm and whimper sulkily 'my wrist is tired'.

If you can't bear the thought of real exercise, don't fret. While stamina is a bonus, you don't have to exert yourself while performing manual sex. If you've ever watched a man masturbate, you'll notice he has it down to a fine energy-conserving art (not surprising after 40,000 hours of training). Some women's idea of a hand job is to throttle his penis at 90mph. Then they get upset when the poor guy smacks their hands away and shouts 'Arrgh'!

To avoid this embarrassing scenario:

- Rub some massage oil on your hands, and — starting from the base of his penis — grasp it firmly but not too tightly, stroke it upwards, smoothly and slowly.
- Use both hands alternately.
- Vary your stroke.
- Again — as with the blow job — pay special attention to the star point.
- Make use of your whole hands: use your fingertips to tease the head in swirly motions, your palms to encircle the shaft and rub up and down, bunch your hands into two fists and slide them up and down his shaft.
- Be firm, but don't choke the poor man.
- Also remember that you are allowed to talk to him during. Talk sexy, tell him how much you're loving this.
- Occasionally stroke his lower stomach, the inside of his thighs, his testicles.
- If possible, try to adopt a non-frenzied facial expression. Admittedly, it's hard work, but the trying-to-work-out-a-complicated-sum-while-on-the-toilet-face doesn't communicate to him that you're enjoying yourself.

Crick Your Neck Fellatio

This is a vulnerable blow-job position which you should only assume if you're certain you want to. It's great for him, less great for you. You lie on the bed, on your back, so that your head is hanging off the edge of the bed. He positions himself in front of your head (so you have a delightful upside-down view of his testicles) and you gently ease the head of his penis into your mouth.

The thrill (to him, anyway) of this crick-your-neck position is that the line of your mouth and throat is straightened so – theoretically – he can make deeper thrusts without choking you. In reality, if you have a strong gag-reflex as soon as the tip of his penis touches the back of your throat, you'll start gagging.

Should you wish, you can dull the reflex by practice – use a dildo if there's the slightest chance your man might thrust too eagerly and/or you might clamp down hard on his penis in a panic to stop the thrusting (should this unfortunate eventuality occur, console yourself with the fact that he deserved it. You told him not to thrust too far. He should have listened).

Even if he promises to restrain himself, hold the base of his penis with one hand to give yourself a degree of control. If, at any time – within the first three seconds or thereafter – you decide it's a no-go, roll over onto your front, and continue giving him an oral treat from a more comfortable position. Like he's going to complain!

Things you should know about this position:

■ You shouldn't attempt if you feel anxious, uncomfortable, or if you've just had a huge dinner.
■ Even if you're happy to try it, the romantic man, the shy man and the tad conservative man might feel uneasy about it – as if it would be treating you badly. The lazy-long-term man might feel the same way, although he may still secretly fancy trying it. The raunchy man will love it.

The Slot Machine

Whereby you barely have to move a muscle and he does all the work. He stands, you kneel down on the floor in front of him, so that his penis is dangling in your face – although if you begin with a few of the earlier techniques, it shouldn't dangle for long. After kissing, licking and fondling his penis, slowly guide it into your mouth. Assume a firm 0-shape with your lips around his shaft, and let him slide in and out. Your head stays still, but your tongue teases and caresses.

The kick for him is that he is in a dominant position. The kick for you is, you are in an idle position. Place a cushion under your knees for comfort. This isn't the first technique to suggest to the lazy long-term man ('You mean I have to stand?') – but the raunchy man, the sensuous man will enjoy it. The romantic man, the shy man and the tad conservative man may hesitate – they worry (as they should) that this is a demeaning technique for a woman. This is only true if he coerces you into doing it and/or never returns the favour. Suggest that to correct the balance, he then gives you oral sex on his knees. Hang on to his head/a wall for support as this delirious experience will make your knees go wobbly.

How to Have Him Begging for More

Optional extras:

- Hold his penis at the base with one hand to give yourself a little control.
- Gently fondle and caress his testicles with your other hand.
- Use a judicious amount of oral suction power to intensify his experience.
- If he does like his prostate being fiddled, now is an excellent time.

Swallow or Duck?

Let's be honest. Chances are, he wants you to swallow. The hypocrite. The average man makes a big fat fuss if a woman doesn't declare his sperm is a tastebud sensation yet if – mouth full of gunk – she hovers menacingly over his mouth, he'll shout NO! and duck away. So, sauce for the goose isn't sauce for the gander. Thus, if you don't want to swallow, don't feel bad about it. If you don't even want his sperm in your mouth – and you don't have to defend your decision because it's your mouth – don't.

Do, however, make a few concessions:

- Make as small a deal as you can of spitting it out. Some men believe that if you reject his sperm, you reject the essence of him. A highly emotive reaction, which may be countered with the question, Well, would you eat my ear wax? On second thoughts, maybe just say Sorry, it's just that I'm full up.
- Maybe do something else erotic with it. Let it spurt on your breasts, and rub it in. (It's apparently great for your skin).
- Don't make any 'urgh' type faces. It's hurtful to him.

- If though, you are happy to swill it merrily round your mouth and swallow in a big, show-offy gulp and smack of your lips, he will probably swoon with joy. Contrary to myth, most men like a woman with a healthy appetite. The raunchy man and the sensuous man will almost expect it (raunchy tends to expect a lot of things because he doesn't understand the phrase 'hang-up'), the lazy long-term man won't believe his luck, the shy man and the romantic man may become tearful with emotion. The unremarkable taste aside, it is a sensual intimate sacrif – sorry – gesture to make.*

* If he's the tad conservative man or the romantic man he might feel guilty because he suspects he's forcing you. Frankly, guilt won't swing it. If you don't want to do something, he shouldn't try to make you, full stop.

Touching Base

The missionary position encourages apathy in a woman and if you're having an off day, it's tempting to contribute only the occasional ah! and feeble push. This little manoeuvre – which has been rather grandly called the coital alignment technique – aims to prevent such disasters. The idea is to arrange yourselves so that the base of his penis rubs against your clitoris as he thrusts. This makes the experience about 40 thousand times more intense for you – and ditto for him.

Specifically, this move is great for the lazy long-term man as it reduces his workload. The excitable new flame, the romantic man, the sensuous man and the raunchy man will appreciate this as it revs up the intensity for you, which delights him, and allows you a more active role in proceedings. The tad conservative man will not have a leg to stand on – he's doing it in his favourite position, what more can he ask for? So:

- assume the missionary position
- let him slip his penis into you
- gently pull him up towards you as if for a kiss, while pushing down against his pubic bone

- shift around till it feels um, ar YES!
- you now start thrusting gently against him until you reach a pace and firmness that suits.

Putting a Bit More Verve into Venue

Your bed is, without doubt, the most comfortable place to have sex. Doing it in the bath, on the kitchen table, in a public toilet, wherever, is awkward and scratchy in comparison. But, for all the awkwardness and scratchiness of silly venues, they are novel, exciting, and therefore a great idea. Meanwhile, if you only have sex in bed, comfortable becomes boring. If – every time you head bedwards – you feel a niggle of 'here we go again – same time, same place' you can bet your bottom he feels the same.

These little techniques will show you how to make the most of any unorthodox venue. Enjoy them – and remember that you can always start canoodling, fiddling, and fondling in an exotic location then progress to the bed midway through proceedings. This applies even if you are a taxi-ride from home: Use the journey to temporarily slow the pace and work up an appetite. Once home, you will fall on each other like two (fabulously good-looking) rhinos on heat.

At your dinner party

Ingredients

- A long tablecloth.
- A prepared-earlier main course.
- A kitchen separate from the dining room.
- Guests who won't bother to come and see if you 'need any help'.

You are going all out to impress, and we're not talking about the food. Choose your sexiest dress and flimsiest underwear (you may, if you wish, forgo the underwear). You want to wow him on sight. Invite at least one guy who your partner is convinced fancies you – a still-friendly ex-boyfriend, your ever-ready platonic male friend – you want to stoke his 'she's-mine!' instinct. Ignore the tedious etiquette that demands you and your partner sit a million miles from each other, and seat your man next to you. You're the host, you're in charge.

Then, while making polite chit-chat with your guests, let your hand creep towards your man's groin and start to get familiar. The tad conservative man, the shy man and the lazy long-term man may actually faint with shock or surprise at this point or, at least, push your hand away. Don't be deterred. Your mission is to give him a raging erection. If you have to unzip his trousers, so much the better. Then, clear the starter plates, demand your man hobbles out to help in the kitchen, and let desire take its course.

Choose your measure of bare-bottomed cheek:

- Leave the kitchen door unlocked.
- Leave the kitchen door slightly ajar.
- Take that bit longer than is strictly polite.

NB this technique can also be performed at someone else's dinner party – although it's advisable to choose the bathroom rather than the kitchen.

How to Have Him Begging for More

Underwater Oral Sex in a Jacuzzi

Outrageous and inconsiderate – but since when has good sex been sensible and magnanimous? Make a morning of it. The first hurdle is to find a municipal sports centre that has a jacuzzi. Or if you are lucky enough to belong to a private health club, turn up at the crack of dawn on a Saturday (sacrifices do have to be made) when the pool area is likely to be deserted. Members of private health clubs are about three million times as likely to complain, and you run the risk of being booted out for rule-breaking.

Anyhow, the advantage of finding a municipal sports centre is that you are anonymous – and the changing rooms are more likely to be mixed. Change into your skimpiest swimsuit or bikini. You might like to have a pre-jacuzzi fondle in your cubicle to get yourselves in the mood. Wear flip-flops or you might get a veruca, and be aware that everyone in the vicinity will know what you're up to as these cubicles are the size of a shoe box but less plush, and your elbows and knees will inevitably rap-bang on the sides.

If, when you enter the jacuzzi, anyone else is in it, you can selfishly encourage them to leave by kissing. The majority of British people cannot stand to be near smooching couples. Once they've huffed and left, you can raise the stakes. This is a test of your man's lung capacity. His mission is to dive underwater, push your bikini bottoms to one side, and give you a little oral lurrrve. Albeit 30 seconds worth.

The raunchy man, the sensuous man and the adventurous man will be tickled pink by this prank, the romantic man may feel uneasy but remind him he's doing you a favour. The lazy long-term man may worry about being spotted – if you've got him to a sports centre the rest is comparatively easy. Meanwhile, the excitable new flame will think Christmas has come (and Christmas won't be the only one). Whatever. When he resurfaces gasping, surreptitiously entice his periscope up, and make him gasp some more.

By the Window

Preferably to be performed at his house — you don't want passers-by to think you live in a place of disrepute. The glee-factor in this little ploy is that anyone who happens to trot by, chances are you are merely leaning out of the window (or pressing against it) and your man has, er, come up behind you to see what you're looking at. You might like to keep your top-half clothed, so that the truth isn't too obvious. Although, the fact that you are both huffing, panting, and shouting 'ooof!' may give them a slight suspicion.

It's simple, but the fact that you are sort of doing it in public is enough to give you both an illicit thrill. You can vary the theme at night by switching off the main lights in your room, stripping off, taking up position, and giving the neighbours something to wonder about. Funnily enough, the lazy long-term man might get a kick out of this one (probably because the neighbours annoyed him by pointing out that his hedge needs cutting).

The excitable new flame, the sensuous man, and the raunchy man will welcome any chance to be saucy. The romantic man will be happiest if you fling open the window and say 'let's make love while looking at the stars'.

The tad conservative man, the shy man might worry about upsetting the neighbours. Tell him that if you make this encounter slow and sensual, they won't notice a thing.

Passnote
Short women might find it useful to wear high heels.

Failnote
His oafish flatmate returning from the pub, glancing up, and shouting 'oy-oy'!

Prompt note
If you think he's more likely to be turned on if he thinks it's his idea, help that idea develop in his head by leaning out of the window half-undressed. As soon as he saunters into the room and claps eyes on your curves, he will — according to an excellent male source — want to pull your knickers down and do it.

Don't you love it when a plan comes together?

The Bath

The bath has a slinky reputation it does not deserve. What is sexy about scraping your knees on the taps, feeling as squashed and bunched up as a concertina, the exertion of having to use the bath handles like a push-up machine to lever yourself up and down, while your bottom wobbles in his face? Of course, it's great for him — he'll love it that your bottom is wobbling in his face. His knees won't be scraping on the taps. He isn't the one having to do aqua-aerobics.

For this reason, although doing it in the bath is awkward, poky, frustrating and exhausting for the woman, most men (under six foot) like the idea. So, even if you use the bath as a sexual appetizer (if the water's hot it will increase blood flow to the penis, but easy does it, don't scald him), and then coax him onto dry land for the rest of the encounter, make sure you know how to make the best of it:

- If your bathroom light is stark and unflattering, use candlelight. Hell, use it anyway.
- Pour some Johnson's Baby Oil into the bath. This will help with lubrication.

- Sit facing each other* and gently use your toes to stroke and explore each other's sensitive bits (make sure your toenails are short and neat otherwise it could go horribly wrong).
- If you have a teeny bath don't feel obliged to go all the way. Wash him all over, slowly work up to his most sensitive part – and let him do the same for you.
- Then, when you're ready to continue on firm ground, wrap yourselves in big fluffy towels (which will of course be heating up on the radiator) and let him carry you into the bedroom. (Make sure all your radiators are working otherwise the mood will dip with the temperature).

* If you want him to go really wild you may have to resign yourself to the tap end.

How to Have Him Begging for More

Shower Power

The shower – and by this I mean a separate enclosed all-on-its-own shower, not a silly attachment to the tap – is about a million times sexier than the bath. For a start, the water isn't stagnating in soapy pools around you, and for a finish, you don't go so crinkly. If he takes a shower with you it should lead to sex as a matter of course. Even if you have a supermarket appointment as a matter of urgency, it is scientifically proven that he will find you hard to resist as:

- You have to get very close indeed for the shower jet to hit you both and no one wants their bottom to get cold.
- Men tend to find wet, shiny, slippery women irresistible – possibly because they look vulnerable? Maybe because they associate it with sexual readiness? Water reminds them of white see-through t-shirts? Who knows – milk it.
- The water pressure sends tingly, invigorating messages to all body parts, unlike the soothingly soporific bath.
- Yet, the line 'Let's have a shower together' sounds off-puttingly bland – even if it does prompt him to shed his

clothes faster than a greased racehorse. Far more seductive to purr, 'I think I'm going to take a long hot, steamy shower' and let him sneak up on you.* Men find the predatory nature of glimpsing the naked outline of a woman behind a shower curtain very exciting. There is that whiff of naughtiness because:

- he's as good as spying on you
- he can choose to slip in and join you
- he can take you by surprise
- he has the treat of soaping you down, the water cascading down and soaking your entwined bodies
- all this wet 'n' wild stuff is most appealing to him.†

* Give yourself a fighting chance – if he's watching a match on tv/playing on his PlayStation don't waste your breath. Choose your moment. Preferably when he's doing the washing up and is angling for some distraction.
† Take it in turns to go down on your knees and give each other an oral treat – the shower adds a wonderful frisson.

Mind Games

As we all know, the sexiest part of the body is the mind (although we buy outrageously expensive bras anyway). Which means that in theory, you should be able to think each other to orgasm. That's the theory. In practice, you can start by playing a simple game. The excitable new flame, the romantic man and the raunchy man will be up for it in all senses. The lazy long-term man and the tad conservative man might need to be bullied, but you'll get there.

Ingredients

- A dice
- A man

The rules

a) You glam up.
b) You sit opposite each other, on the floor.
c) You watch each other for five minutes, and think arousing thoughts about the other person. E.g. what you'd like to do to them, your favourite body part, where they

like to be tickled. No touching. Ideally, your arousal level will go up a notch.

d) Then, you throw a dice. Whoever gets the highest number dictates a piece of clothing that the other should remove. Each throw the dice three times, or you'll never get anywhere.*

e) Another five minutes sexy contemplation.

f) Throw the dice again. This time, whoever gets the highest score dictates what body part their partner should massage, for a minute. (i.e., the loser has to massage him or herself). The aim – to put on a bit of a show.

g) Keep throwing the dice until you are both panting.

h) Bit more contemplation.

i) Throw the dice. Whoever gets the highest score is allowed to touch their partner wherever they choose, with their tongue, for no more than thirty seconds.

j) Repeat – alternate contemplation, clothing removal, 30 second touching – if you're doing it right, there'll come a point where you're both so white hot, you can't stick to the rules any longer.

---

* If you're very patient, you can string it out for as long as you can stand.

At work

Great for the raunchy man, the excitable new flame, the sensuous man, the mischievous man.

Tricky, controversial, and all the saucier for it. Let's assume you work at the same office. There are a few small difficulties you may have to overcome, such as:

- your colleagues
- your boss
- security guards
- security cameras.

As Ellen and Jeremy discovered. Ellen says, 'Jeremy was working as a barrister and he had a little office at the top of the building, with a beautiful view onto a park – and a lockable door. I went to visit him one afternoon and we started kissing and got carried away. We were having sex when we heard a stomping of feet – someone was coming up the stairs. Whoever it was started knocking on the door, and kept twisting the knob. We had our knickers round our ankles! Finally he gave up and went downstairs. Then we heard him announce: "Ellen and Jeremy are having sex!!" Jeremy was so horrified, everything collapsed! Later, I went downstairs sheepishly and snuck out! When Jeremy ventured downstairs everyone laughed uproariously at him. He now works elsewhere.'

If you are determined to have sex at work – and don't want everyone to find out – full-on cheek is required. Working late together is the obvious ploy, but getting down to hanky-panky in an open-plan office is risky – there's always a security guard plodding through his rounds, or someone dashing back at 10.30pm because they left their house keys on their desk. The alternative? Be brazen. Quietly approach your manager with the legitimate excuse that you need to hold a private meeting re. a client/budgeting/finances etc. but because of your many responsibilities it will have to be squeezed in after hours (heh heh). Furthermore, you need a quiet private room where you won't be disturbed and a big table so you can spread out (heh heh again). The boardroom? Perfect! (Alas, you may actually have to hold the meeting post-coitally, otherwise everyone will wonder about your unfinished business).

Garden Party

Unless you are overlooked by a police station, the garden is a fabulous venue – legitimately outdoors but near enough to the house so that if you need to pee you can nip to a comfortable carpeted bathroom rather than crouch amid a thatch of stinging nettles.

However, if you are dealing with the tad conservative man you may have to – as one woman did – train him slowly but surely. When they did it, they did it in bed. Then, one day she boldly hijacked him on the stairs. He was unwilling, but she insisted. Their next bonk took place in bed. Then, a week or so later, she ambushed him in the lounge, the kitchen, the conservatory and finally, triumphantly – the garden. She says, 'I think the neighbours saw, but so what?' Quite. Who wants to admit they're a Peeping Tom?

However – if he's still resisting:

■ Pitch a real or makeshift tent – maintaining you just want to play Wendy House. Then, once you're in there, throw yourself at him. A tent renders the nosy neighbour excuse invalid, and is especially fun if it's raining (if you have lots of blankets, and your groundsheet is secure).

■ Lure him outside on the premise of fresh air. Choose a summer's evening when it's warm, dark, and the lawn isn't boglike. Say 'let's lie on the grass and gaze at the moon.' Then pounce.

The conservative man will soon learn to enjoy it *al fresco*. Meanwhile, the excitable new flame, the adventurous man, and the romantic man will need no persuading. Give the lazy long-term man a choice between the park or the garden. He'll choose the garden, because it has closer access to the fridge. But great! He's chosen to have sex in the garden!

Park Pranks

A park or a heath may be far away from all mod cons but it is thrillingly risque. Should the primal urge take you in the middle of the day, give yourself a fighting chance of not being arrested and seek out a Weeping Willow, preferably amid the most picturesque surroundings you can think of. Check he doesn't get hayfever. Remove as few clothes as possible – should a park warden approach you can make a quick getaway. If you can bear to, wear a floaty dress. The romantic man will be so knocked out by this concession to 'femininity,' he'll be hot to trot.

As ever, the excitable new flame will be happy to oblige anywhere. The lazy long-term man may have to be enticed into the remote countryside as, frankly, he finds the thought of being caught with his pants down horrific. The tad conservative man, the shy man will be terrified that a colleague will spot him – warm him up by plying him with seductive words and a little beer. Just this once, you may resort to reading love poetry. The point is to introduce him to the concept that making love is an exotic adventure. Liberate him from his prim limitations, his sexual ego rockets, and you secure a special place in his heart and trousers.

The next step: fun as it is to break the law in broad daylight, it's even more tantalising to sneak into a park or heath at night as:

- It's spookily dark and every crackling twig gives you an excuse to squeal and clutch each other.
- You're breaking even more laws by scrambling over railings when the park is shut (and he gets a chance to peek up your skirt – a childish pleasure that men retain from nursery school).
- It is an adventure, and men are turned-on by women who, rather than whinging about their chipped nails, are up for it, in every sense.

How to Have Him Begging for More

Table Tennis

Sex on the kitchen table – or if you're feeling flash – the dining room table tends to give both parties involved a sense of pride and satisfaction. It's so, dammit, spontaneous! And why is it spontaneous? Because no one in their right mind would ever plan to make love on a hard wooden slab. If you've ever had the misfortune to lie on your back on a table while your man merrily pumps away and your coccyx digs painfully into the unyielding surface, you'll know that it's impossible to concentrate, let alone enjoy, because on each thrust you're thinking 'ow!' 'ow!' and wondering if your bruising will turn purple.

Yet – you hate to break up the party. So don't. Instead, use the following tips to ensure that your table-top shenanigans are fantastic and pain-free:

- If he shows a penchant for doing it on tables, start keeping the odd cushion on the chair so that, should he ease you into the missionary position, you can grab it and place it at the small of your back – no interruption, no fuss. Incidentally, raising your hips enables him to thrust more deeply. So everyone's happy.

- Go for the doggy position – either both clamber onto the table (grab onto the edges for support) or stand on the floor, bending over the table, with him behind you. This way, the table features in proceedings, but doesn't booby trap them.

- Or, try this one: he stands at the table's edge, you lie on your side on the table (cushion under your hip so you're not crippled) making an L-shape. Your legs (the horizontal line of the L) should run parallel to the edge of the table. Then he can just slip it in.

- Even better – make yourself comfortable, and grandly allow him to eat you off the table. Well, isn't that what it's for?

How to Have Him Begging for More

Deeper and Deeper

Certain positions, like doggy, are great for deep penetration but give the woman no control. So, if your man thrusts too fiercely it can be painful. This friendlier, intimate, unabashed position, allows him deep, satisfactory penetration, but also ensures you an equal measure of control. The bonus – he'll be rubbing against exquisitely sensitive places so expect duvet-shattering results. Perfect for every man (what's not to like?).

■ Start off making love in the missionary position.
■ Curl your legs and hoick them back so your knees are adjacent to your ears.
■ Let's rock!

Sex Sensation!

You have five senses – and if you make the most of them during sex, the experience becomes a glorious inspirational rainbow of sunshiny feelings and sensual delight, rather than a grey mundane clunking better-than-doing-the-vacuuming pastime. It is so easy to be lazy during sex – which is why a little effort goes a long way. All men – lazy long-term, excitable new flame, tad conservative, raunchy man – will be inordinately impressed if you gently emphasize even one sense when you make love. Let's begin with smell.

The first thing to be said about smell is – hooray, an excuse to pamper ourselves. Certainly, there has been a lot of waffle written about pheremones – the natural scent secreted by people and wolves (or something) that is supposed to drive us all crazy with lust. While your natural scent is an integral part of why he fancies you, an occasional blast from the beauty counter can also work wonders. Don't trust yourself to know what he likes. On the pretext of buying a new game for his PlayStation, go to a large store, walk through the cosmetics department and on the spur of the moment decide to buy yourself some perfume and request his opinion. There's got to be something that has a riotous effect on his hormones.

Then, when you return home — and he's had at least three hours of twiddling about on his computer — have a long indulgent bath then, when your body is still a little damp, dab a little perfume in all the places you would like to be kissed. A particularly good sensual spot is an inch and a half directly below your belly button. Then sling on a flimsy something and waft past him.

As nature takes its course and your temperature soars, he will be treated to delicious whiffs of Chanel's *Allure* + You, and as he hungrily breathes it in, it makes his experience headier.*

---

* Smell is a powerful mind-cue, and within weeks, whenever he gets a waft of that perfume, he will dream of delightful romps with delicious you.

Touch

Unless you're a genius, you probably touch him quite a bit during sex without even thinking about it. Rather like looking in the rear-view mirror when driving. This time, your easy-peasy mission is to concentrate on and be aware of your sensations, and ask him to do the same. Make a deal of it. Go shopping (any excuse), head straight to the haberdashery department, and decide together if you want to make blindfolds out of red velvet or white silk.... Then ask the assistant to measure you out a few strips. Don't feel obliged to say what it's for. The assistant will probably guess.

The conservative man and the shy man may feel terribly daring, bless them. Say it's not frivolous, it's necessary — you don't want him to be distracted. The romantic man will love the idea of velvet, although he may insist on blue for himself. The excitable new flame probably won't be able to resist dropping heavy innuendoes in front of the assistant. Whatever turns him on. The lazy long-term man will be happy to take part, as long as you forgo the shopping trip and dig out a scarf from the hall cupboard. The raunchy man and the sensuous man will go along with anything.

Don't gabble on the way home. Just smile dirtily at him. Let him simmer. By the time you unlock the front door, he will be gibbering with impatience. Take him to the bedroom, undress each other, then gently blindfold him and lay him down on the bed. Then, don't touch him at all – just blow gently at select areas of his body. Then do some licking. Progress to sucking. Trail your fingers on an exploratory journey from his head to his toes. Rub your nipples on his chest – and elsewhere. Ask him to tell you what he's feeling (don't be too surprised if what he's feeling is 'Ah! Arrh! Oof! Wow!').

Seeing Stars One

A simple rule, this: regard yourself as a beautiful present to be slowly (or frenziedly) unwrapped. If, when sex is imminent, you and he undress yourselves at opposite sides of the bed – you patiently undoing your cardigan buttons, him slowly untying his shoe laces – stop right there. What are you, pensioners? Next time hanky panky is on the cards, if his hand dares wander towards his own zip, gently place it on yours. He'll understand. Shockingly, even the romantic man may have abandoned this basic mood-setting habit. Re-acquaint him with it.

It imbues the atmosphere with an anticipatory tingle of specialness. It makes him look at you and imagine the pleasure you and he are going to give each other. Considering that men are so feted as visual creatures, it is remarkable how slapdash they often become about feasting their eyes on their gorgeous woman. What woman hasn't nearly bankrupted herself on some candy floss spider spun lingerie, only to have it go unnoticed because her partner was footling along in a daze? Make him notice you.

Best to undress:

- A many-buttoned dress/shirt.
- Real stockings and suspenders (the yearly sacrifice is enough).
- A foolproof-hook bra.
- Drawstring/zipped/button trousers.

Worst to undress:

- A polo-neck (your head gets stuck).
- Tights.
- Elasticated trousers.

Seeing Stars Two

If, for some inexplicable reason he doesn't swing into the habit of undressing you – a tall order for the lazy long-term man, admittedly – don't revert to yanking off your clothes yourself, willy-nilly. Show him what he's missing. Make him yearn to get his hands on you. Tease him. Taunt him. Strip for him. You can either go for the whole caboodle – complete with pinging your knickers at him via a high-kick to a soundtrack of *New York New York* – or a more understated slipping-garments-slowly-off sophistication.

Practise in front of the mirror first – to music if you prefer – until you feel confident.

Tips to strip:

- Do yourself a favour and don't wear a polo neck sweater (see above).
- It's easier when you're wearing a skirt rather than trousers.
- You can either stun your prey with a steady, provocative gaze, or tantalize him by a coy downward cast look (choose whether you want him to feel powerful or powerless).

How to Have Him Begging for More

- Once you've undone your shirt, button by button, slip one sleeve off your shoulder, smoothing your upper arm with your fingers (making him wish they were his fingers).
- Slowly slowly, shrug off the other sleeve, so both your shoulders are bare. You want him to gawp at each body part as you reveal it.
- Shrug out of the shirt fully, keeping hold of it with one hand. Then, should you fancy, you can give it a short twirl before casting it aside (make sure it doesn't hit him in the face).
- Slowly unzip your skirt, do a little wriggle, and let it fall to the ground. Daintily step out of it.
- Strike a provocative pose – hands on hips, pouty lips (think pouty pop stars).
- You will have donned your highest heels for this occasion – they make your legs go on forever, even if you're five foot two. Kick them off.
- If you are wearing stockings – superb. Undo one, and roll it down, inch by inch. Bend over so your bottom sticks out, but keep your back straight. Smooth your hands over your skin to remind him of the delights to come.
- String it out. Don't rush to divest yourself of your underwear. Tease him.
- Invite him to remove your knickers with his teeth.

Tantric Sex, abridged

You're busy people. (Unless you're students). You and he probably don't have a whole day spare to indulge in wall-to-wall sex. Fine. You don't have to put 24 hours aside. Let's compromise on five. The point of Tantric sex is to bring your souls together — as well as your bits — in an overwhelming fusion of mind and body. It is awesome, powerful, spiritual sex — and if you want to have him hooked, lusting after you while he's at work, thinking sniffily 'She's not a patch on my woman' when he spies Elle McPherson in an advert — it is something you should try out.

Importantly, he doesn't have to maintain an erection the whole time, so it's easy street for him. This incentive apart, Tantric sex will give your lazy long-term man a stunning reminder of just one of the reasons you're together, wow the raunchy man — who is probably too impatient to have tried this before but willing to give it a go, and bliss out the romantic man, the sensuous man — you may both end up crying with emotion. Tell the tad conservative man that it doesn't involve any implements, and that you'll video *Newsnight*.

The excitable new flame may find this a bit full-on — be wary: if he's one of those men who is tediously prone to thinking that every woman who sleeps with him wants to trap him into marriage, this may give him the wrong idea (or the right one). Also, if this is a lust-match, rather than a love match, you might not want your minds to connect. That said, you can pitch it to him as a fun game called 'Watch the Earth Move'.

Ten Steps of Tantric Sex

- Book a hotel for the occasion. Oh go on. Just one night. You want your surroundings to be clean, calm, and tidy, don't you? Order mineral water and fruit on room service — at least, that's what the experts advise but as you are supposed to enjoy this, I advise champagne and chocolate mousse. Your own supplies should include scented candles, and meditative music, and anything else you fancy. The following should take you approximately five hours — but feel free to string it out for longer.

- Take a bath together. Draw the curtains. Light the candles.

- Sit on the bed or floor, back to back with your partner. Don't speak. Shut your eyes, and allow your breathing to fall in synch with his. Be aware of his breathing. Stay put for a few minutes.

- Then face each other. Gaze into each other's eyes and put your hand on each other's heart, feeling the beat. Still breathe together.

- Rub your own palms together to generate warmth (he should do the same). Then touch all ten fingertips to his.

Do this for about a minute. Note: you should be smiling at each other.

- Then kiss. Breathe. Kiss. Gaze. Touch fingers. Nothing naughtier for at least an hour.
- He should be rigid with excitement. Make him lie down. You climb on top. Let him enter you – but only one inch. Try to keep still (you can clench your pelvic muscles to help maintain his erection). If you or he gets too excited, stop.
- Choose another position, but no more than an inch of penetration is allowed. Keep gazing, touching, breathing together. Stop, if you think you're close to orgasm.
- Have a break – drink water or Krug, feed each other fruit or mousse. Don't be tempted to turn on the television.
- Try another position – as long as you maintain eye contact, the choice is yours. Touch, breathe, and possibly, maybe allow him to go all the way. If he doesn't have the most almighty orgasm he's ever experienced – you'll just have to try again tomorrow.

The Big Dipper

Great for the sensuous man, the romantic man, the raunchy man, the excitable new flame, the lazy long-term man.

This is one of the techniques you can use in Tantric sex – but when you don't have time, you can use it for plain old earthbound sex too. It's such a tease, but it teaches your man that good things come to those who wait. Trouble is, most men hate to wait. They are what the experts call 'goal directed'. They haven't the patience to flimflam around. No pussyfooting for them! They want to cut to the chase. Consequently, sex lasts for 15 minutes.

Then, belatedly, he realises that although he's got what he wanted, it wasn't nearly as good as it was in his head. Why? Because you the woman, barely had your knickers off before it was over. You didn't have a chance to become properly aroused. The big dipper ensures that you both simmer just below boiling point for at least, w o h! twenty minutes. How? Only permit him shallow thrusts.

Your vagina entrance is rich with nerve endings, and extremely sensitive to stimulation. So let him stimulate. Tantalize him (and yourself) by gripping his penis and stroking your labia with it. Let him dip in a little and out. Ignore all begging and whinging. Silence him with a kiss. The longer you make him wait, the more explosive the results when you finally permit him to go all the way.

What to say to stop him rushing:

- I thought big boys lasted longer.
- This technique leads to an earth-shattering orgasm.
- After this, we have to do the housework.

The Duchess 69

A kinky little way to freshen up an old favourite. The 69 position is beautifully erotic, but also pretty intimate, and some women recoil from it as it makes them feel too exposed. They wonder what exactly he's thinking as their vagina blocks out his sunlight. (Hint: unless he's a mutton-head deadbeat who doesn't deserve the honour, he's probably thinking 'mmm'). However, if you'd like to vary the theme, the Duchess 69 is a cute one to try.

Lie head to toe, but on your sides. Instead of the usual, lick then suck on each other's toes. (If they've been encased in shoes and socks all day, it's your prerogative to wash each other's feet first – which in itself can be a sensual experience). As you are paying oral homage to each other's tootsies, let your hands wander to his groin if he's got more than one braincell, his hand will soon creep to yours. The tad conservative man may find this one odd, but surprisingly likeable. The excitable new flame, the mischievous man will enjoy this new way of exploring your heavenly body.

The raunchy man, the sensous man will wonder why he didn't think of this, and the lazy long-term man will smilingly recall how he used to like having his feet tickled. It's a winner!

Pre-toe-sucking preparation:

- Cut your toenails so there are no jagged edges.
- Paint toenails in a sexy hue.
- If your feet are callused, consider a pedicure (pampering ahoy!).
- Moisturize, but not too much as it tastes horrible.

The Big Squeeze

Kegels sound like a type of East European biscuit. In fact, they are boring exercises that new mothers do to strengthen their vaginal muscles after a great big baby has squeezed through and stretched them slack. Certainly, you have better things to do with your spare time, but if you practise clenching and relaxing – as if you were trying to stop peeing mid-flow – your vaginal muscles will strengthen and tighten. Then – when he's merrily pumping away, you can give him a very pleasant surprise indeed. Hold the clench to increase the friction.

This technique can be used on any man – the romantic man may be taken aback but mightily impressed. The raunchy man, the sensuous man will think 'Wahey! More power to the elbow!' (or similar). The lazy long-term man will probably grin with pleasure and whisper where have you been all my life? And, the excitable new flame might very well think the same thing. The tad conservative man and the shy man will just count their lucky stars. Kegel exercises are especially useful if you ever become very wet and lose friction. They are also useful if his penis is not very thick. Whatever the circumstances – he'll be grateful. So perfect, then apply at will.

The Multiple Male Orgasm

The Loafer has got to do some work for this one. My god, you can't do everything! The lazy long-term man needs a bit of exercise, so this one is perfect for him. It also works well on the raunchy man, the adventurous man, the sensuous man, and any man with a shred of patience. Yet unless your excitable new flame is truly laid back, he might be a little frightened if you suggest this on the second date. Say pleasantly, 'Well, if you don't want a multiple orgasm, that's your choice'. He'll grovel. But if he wants to reap the reward, he has to do some hard labour.

Here's how:

- It is now his turn to exercise his pelvic muscles. If anything, it will make him appreciate your efforts. The technique is the same – he must clench, hold, and relax the muscles that control his urine-flow. (They will – eventually – also allow him to control ejaculation).
- Take him to bed and take it to the max! Just before he is about to orgasm, stop him. (Don't, please, use the panic technique – which is to smack his penis sharply on its head). There are kindlier methods – the easiest is to pull

gently down on his testicles. If you prefer, you can squeeze his penis firmly, just below the head, holding for about half a minute. This prevents the sperm from spurting.

- Get back to what you were doing. Every time he approaches orgasm, apply either of the above techniques.

- In theory (it may take some practising – excellent) during this process he should start having non-ejaculatory orgasms. If he is relaxed and confident enough (don't yank his balls too hard) he may have a series of them – the intensity of which will leave him dizzy with joy. (Even if he doesn't manage a multiple orgasm initially, he's still likely to experience a more powerful solo orgasm than usual as you've delayed the moment).

The Sex Slave

Fabulous this, as it means you get to live the life of Riley, while he gets to live the life of Baldrick. Men love to be bossed, although he may need time to acclimatize to the idea. Mention it once – 'Sweetheart, there's a sex game I know that would really turn me on. It is …' – then shut up about it. Two weeks later, when he's had time to ponder, mention it again. Don't nag. (It's unlikely that you'll need to). It may be wise to wait a while before suggesting this to your excitable new flame – not that he'll think you're weird, he'll panic that you're a woman who insists the man does her ironing too.

The lazy long-term man will need bribing – tell him you can swop roles the next time and you promise not to complain even if washing his car is part of it (just lie, basically). The raunchy man, the sensuous man will be game for a laugh (and it is a laugh). The tad conservative man, the shy man may resist so tell him you'll be gentle with him. As for the romantic man, reassure him that it's partly a ruse to get him to bring you breakfast in bed. Now! He has to abide by the rules. He is submissive to your every whim – any show of independence results in a spanking.

Note

Some people find spanking violently arousing. Others cannot see the point. So if you cannot see the point, show your displeasure any way you like. Squirt some whipped cream at him, throw the washing up gloves at him, make him lick your foot – you're the boss! (He should call you something appropriate. You can call him 'Slave'). Here, as a mere taster, is an example timetable. Please expand on it, add whips – leather or walnut – chains – steel or daisy, whatever turns you on:

- 9.30am he rings your doorbell.
- 9.31am he brings you breakfast in bed (you should be arrayed in your finest lingerie). Breakfast should be highly feedable food.
- 9.50am–3pm he does the housework.
- 9.51am he runs away – okay, okay – he doesn't do the housework, he just washes up the breakfast things and runs you a bubble bath.
- 10am he tests the bathwater, undresses you, and gently lowers you into the bath (NB all instructions you give him should be delivered in an imperious tone).
- 10.01–10.30am he washes you, every bit, including your hair.
- 10.30–10.40am he dries you with the warm towel he has put to heat on the radiator.
- 10.40 am he carries you back to bed.
- 10.41am he has to strip for you – like he means it, no juvenile giggling.

- 10.50am–12noon he has to pleasure you. And if he dares say 'What do you mean?' snap back 'Use your imagination! – and call me Madam!' Penetration is vetoed.
- 12–1pm he prepares lunch, and feeds it to you.
- 1–2pm you nap while he clears up.
- 2pm you summon him to your bedside again (should you wish, you can buy handcuffs from Agent Provocateur, and take him for a walk. The thrill is – will anyone notice, and big fat hairy deal if they do. Good luck in persuading him. If he refuses, you can always handcuff him to the oven door for a while).

The Rocking Chair

This is a beautiful position that the romantic man, the sensuous man and the lazy long-term man will both adore. The romantic man will be in heaven because you stare into each other's eyes. The lazy long-term man will rate it because you're sitting down. The tad conservative man will think it's super (you're sitting on his lap, all is as it should be etc). The raunchy man, the shy man and the new-ish flame might find it a bit too intimate, but if you think he's ready to take the relationship onto a more soulful level, then this is one way of doing it.

How To

a Pinpoint a comfortable chair — no bony old wooden things.* Go for maximum padding.

b Undress him, let him undress you, and do whatever it takes to get him aroused.

c When he is erect, sit him in the chair, and climb on so you're facing him. If the chair has arms, hook your legs

---

* If you own a cat, shut it out of the room. The testers for this technique had to abandon ship as another pussy joined in by making a lunge for lazy long-term man's bottom through a hole at the back of the chair.

over them. Your bodies should be touching, you should be looking into each other's eyes. Insert his penis, but no pumping. Both of you keep still.

d Then hug each other, and gently rock back and forth. Kiss as much as you like. Don't close your eyes. Keep looking at each other.

e Don't worry if his erection subsides, keep rocking, keep kissing, and it's sure to return.

The Ultimate Vanity

Doing it with mirrors is a monstrous turn-on for some men – usually those who enjoy running on treadmills like hamsters and wearing tight t-shirts. Others – usually those who feel faint at the mention of the word 'exercise' and have to eat a Big Mac to recover – will become grumpy, irritable, and shrivelly if they so much as catch a glance of their naked reflection. So, the usual man categories don't apply here. However, whatever their measure of shyness concerning their own body, most men get off on seeing their woman in all her reflected glory, so gather as many large mirrors as you can lay your hands on.

Remember the mirror is your friend:

■ Don't panic about unflattering angles. If you're having a good time, he'll have seen them already.
■ Don't keep glancing nervously at the mirror. Any look should be pouting, and confident. So catch his eye and camp it up. If you don't feel it, fake it.*

---

* Please note – fake confidence, nothing else

- If you and he feel too exposed, opt for doing it in front of a half-length mirror (the one over the bathroom sink?) rather than the full-length wardrobe type.
- If you and he feel desperate for exposure, unhook a mirror from the wall, find somewhere to do it standing up (rear entry, you bent over the kitchen table/holding onto the bathroom sink) and place the mirror on the floor beneath your feet.
- The most devious mirror is the sort you can tilt (as they do in store changing rooms to make you look taller and thinner). Tilt away.

Look Darling, No Hands!

Making love with your hands tied forces you to be more inventive with all the other bits of your body. Tie his. The romantic man will think this impossibly sexy. The raunchy man will love it for its tantalising nature. The lazy long-term man might run out of willpower after four minutes and demand that manual power be reinstated. Ignore. The excitable new flame will be driven crazy with lust (tell him to get used to it). The tad conservative man should like it too – what's not to like? If he can't bear to be restrained (unlikely) let him tie yours.

If his hands are tied – unless you own handcuffs, a scarf will suffice – use the opportunity to tease him mercilessly. You may either tie them together behind his back or above his head, or attach him to the bedpost so he's half spread-eagled (consider beforehand how mobile you need him to be). Let him learn to use his mouth to touch, taste, lick, nibble, nip, suck and kiss on all parts of your body. Just make those parts easily available to him. But not that easily. If you want him to suck your nipple, don't just plonk it in his mouth. Use it to tickle him in the near vicinity.

You have the advantage so use it. Do whatever you like – from sitting on his face to nuzzling his ear to drizzling pools of massage oil on his groin and torso and slip-sliding your whole delightful self up and down it. He will be ravenous to connect, and not just with your obvious bits. He can't use the easy option and paw you. So, he'll be obliged to engage his whole body in making love to you. He can rub himself up against you, stroke you with his toes, lick that delicate spot at the back of your neck – the possibilities are endless.

Holiday Frolics

Pooling your resources – If you have a private pool, or belong to a health club and are prepared to jump out of bed at the crack of dawn, you can indulge in this particular water sport all year round. Otherwise, use it to make your summer break abroad rather more special. Just don't choose a hotel where the dining room has portholes with an underwater view of the outdoor pool – or your sex life will be less of a fiesta than a fiasco.

Making It Happen

■ Entice him into the water – the lazy long-term man may have to be forced, the raunchy man will dive in eagerly, the tad conservative man may need coaxing – (pretend you just want to play softball, heh heh).* Ideally you will be wearing a bikini rather than a costume. (If you own the private pool you need wear nothing at all, unless

---

*Don't want to be a killjoy, but as condoms aren't exactly great protection underwater, this might not be the kind of jape you want to indulge in with an Excitable New Flame or a holiday Romeo.

you feel he ought to unwrap you like a present whatever the circumstance).

- Do whatever it takes to get each other excited, then lure him to the shallow end. Ideally, the water should be at his crotch level.
- Then wriggle out of your bikini bottoms, and wrench off his shorts (if he's the romantic man then maybe peel them off gently).
- Then – and here's the fun bit – climb onto his erect penis and wrap your legs around his waist.
- Tell him to gently bend and straighten his knees as he thrusts in and out. Once you get into a rhythm, the gentle pressure of the water lapping at your sensitive bits will make you realize what holidays are all about.

The Jetsetter

Ingredients

- One man, preferably tanned.
- One jacuzzi, or pool with strong jets.

You can do this in Britain, but it's so much more fun out-doors. Heaven forbid anyone sees you – such behaviour is judged on a par with peeing in a pool. The raunchy man, the sensuous man, the mischievous man will be well up for it. The tad conservative man, the shy man may initially wimp out – don't suggest this the minute you arrive. Give him a week or so to chill out first. The romantic man may fancy it more if you suggest creeping out at midnight. (Cover your top halves in mosquito repellent – it may not taste nice, but the alternative, being covered in red itchy blotches, is even worse).

- Tell him you want to cool off. Maybe invite him to join you in the poolside shower first.
- Climb into the pool at the shallow end. Face the jet,

standing with your legs apart. Hold onto the side for support, and draw up your knees.

- Your beloved stands behind you, and slips in his erect member.
- Ideally, the whoosh of the underwater jet should provide your clitoris and his testicle area with the treat of their lives.

Step To It

Simple but effective.

a You slink into the pool – shallow end as usual.
b Undress.
c Arouse.
d Grab onto a pool step at surface level with both hands, and float on your stomach.
e He kneels down/stands behind you and pops his penis in. (Find your own level). Again, you both benefit from the movement of the water over your non-suntanned bits. (You can use stairs on dry land for similar fun. Except don't bother trying to float. If you're pining for real sunlight and foreign climes, smother each other in suntan oil first).

Beach Bunny

The vast majority of men are big of mouth, quaking of trouser. Of course they want to do it on the beach, but fear of getting sand in their pecker or a bullet in their buttocks courtesy of beach security may turn them chicken. The tad conservative man, the shy man and the lazy long-term man will have to be psyched up (you'll have less trouble with the excitable new flame, raunchy man, sensuous man and romantic man). Here's how to make the dream happen with no casualties:

- Suss out what beaches are best for hanky-panky — preferably at the stage of booking your destination.
- Once you're there, if it doesn't just happen, beautifully, romantically, under the stars, waves lapping at your toes while he laps a bit further up, then plan it.
- Do a bit of low-key scouting (your darling needn't know — better to surprise him). Check which beaches aren't patrolled, are safe.
- Hotfoot it to the beach of choice, relax, sunbathe, smooch, get in the mood. If you're doing it in broad daylight, choose a good vantage point — if anyone does

turn up you can roll out of sight. If you're doing it at night, spray yourselves with insect repellent.

- If necessary, pitch a windbreak.
- If you're eschewing your beach blanket, better that you go on top – or you'll both end up with painfully sandpapered bits. The End.

How to Have Him Begging for More

Figure of Eight

Quick Fix

Sometimes during sex, the woman gets too wet and the man can't feel anything. Funny – he may be romantic, conservative, excitable new, lazy long-term, or raunchy – but he never considers the option that his penis might be less than gargantuan. Never mind. You're too wet and he can't feel anything.

To achieve more friction he should:

- Use slower strokes, each time nearly withdrawing. You can grab the base of his penis and hold it as he thrusts into you.
- Thrust in an imaginary figure of eight (8).
- Take a five minute breather from penetration and do other sexy things. If he's gone squidgy and sulkily withdraws because he can't feel anything (alright already!) ignore him, and play with another part of his body. His penis will recover in time.

Shutting Your Legs

Simple, slinky, surprisingly effective. Sexperts often suggest it if his penis is a tad short, but it's great whatever his size. He goes on top, you take it easy. As he penetrates, shut your legs, squeezing your thighs tightly together. This position helps his penis to rub your clitoris as it goes – and it also gives him a sensation of tightness. Well, he's not going to complain, is he?

Attitude Techniques

You can be technically brilliant in the sack, but leave him cold if you lack self-confidence, try to be what you're not, act on preconception rather than intuition. Your attitude is your charisma – and going through the motions, however proficiently, is not enough. When you are confident enough to know that you deserve as much pleasure as you can take, and thoroughly relish taking it, that's when sex turns into a magic experience. Your man will sense those vibes – and he'll want to be part of the feeling. It will take his lovemaking experience to the next level – he won't be able to stay away.

Fluent Sex talk

Great for all men!

Contrary to myth, it is not essential to be a gutter mouth to excite your man during sex. Do not feel that you have to spout filth if, normally, your most outrageous expletive is 'for goodness sake!' If it is, when you attempt to talk dirty you will sound hideously embarrassed – and it will show, which makes you both feel silly. If you sense that he's really aching for you to let rip with the filth, then try roaring, 'ooh! Harder!' Sorry, but if you feel uncomfortable using four letter words, then he'll have to make do with that.

What you can do – which is far sexier than shouting self-consciously about stiff cocks – is to show him exactly what you want. Place your hand on his, and put it where you want it to be. This way, you can show him the speed and pressure you like, without having to give complicated instructions.

You can, of course, say, 'I love it when you do this,' (manual demonstration). But always couch your requests in positive terms, e.g. 'That's nice, but I prefer it when you do this.' And remember: there is nothing more alluring to men than a woman who knows what she likes, and isn't afraid to ask for it. It is immensely frustrating for him to have to guess what his lover likes (and the same goes for you). But if you show each other, he knows he can ask for what he likes too, and everyone is more than happy.

Incidentally, during sex never say to him:

■ Oh my liddle bay-bee, you're so cute!
■ Oh my liddle bay-bee, it's so cute!
■ Is it in yet?
■ That was quick.
■ You've got an infected spot – shall I pop it?

Never say about yourself:

■ I feel a bit sick – I think I'm still digesting.
■ My stomach isn't usually this round – it must be wind.
■ Don't look at my bum, it's massive!
■ Oh don't go down there, let me wash first!*

You will never, ever have a man begging for more if you belittle yourself. Mini pep talk: If he wants to have sex with you, you don't have to be Sherlock Holmes to decipher that this probably means that he finds you attractive.

* Oh for pity's sake. Has he a mental age of 14? Have you? If you're that bothered and you haven't washed for a week, then you should suggest having a bath together first. Otherwise, grow up and realize that sex is about musky, natural smells, and squeaky clean is about operating theatres.

Now. Cast your mind back to when you first met. Did you attract him by moaning 'oh my bottom is awful' or did you attract him by being your rather wonderful, entertaining, funny, chirpy self? Probably the latter. Therefore: why should he continue being attracted to you if you stop doing those wonderful entertaining things – and start doing other, pointless, tedious things?

Also, when a man pays a compliment voluntarily, it's worth something. If he says it because he thinks he is being prompted, it's worth nothing. In fact, it's a negative thing. No one likes to be manipulated. Anyhow, if you are nasty about yourself, soon enough he'll believe you – and leave you.

The Early Morning Pounce

Great for the sensuous man, the raunchy man, the romantic man, not great for the knackered man.

Setting your alarm half an hour earlier for sex is a bum deal. You are roused from deep sleep, you open unfocused eyes, blearily peer at the alarm clock, regard his snoring form, think 'sod that for a laugh' and fall unconscious.

Ideal Scenario

Set your alarm for the usual time, and resolve to skip breakfast/do your make up on the train. Which leaves you with a spare ten minutes. That's all you need. Drrrrrrringgggg! At this point, your man will still be sweetly dreaming. Nip into the bathroom and brush your teeth first. (He will be less impressed if your teeth are like suede and your mouth smells like a badger's lair. As for the state of his mouth – see notes below).

Quietly lift the sheet away, take his penis in your hands, and rub it to erection. (Some men make the job easier with a fine display of morning glory). Once his penis is stiff, gently climb aboard, and slowly ease yourself up and down. Depending on your degree of gentleness, he'll ease out of the most incredible dream into an even better one.

Swot Note
If you are a real show off, you can do this at 3am, should you happen to wake up. Men love it, because it's cheeky and it's surprising.

Maybe Not Note
If he's lazy long-term man he may not be quite so chuffed as he should be, because he needs at least nine hours sleep and hates to be woken up. Perhaps this technique is best avoided on a Sunday night, or if he has an important meeting the following day.

Bare Bot Note
Men who have happy relationships and a great sex life perform far better at work, and are less stressed than those who aren't getting any. So if you do decide to go ahead, you'll very probably make his day.

Sex Tip
For the Thorough Woman
Avoid garlicky or spicy foods for the previous two days. Floss your teeth the night before, so you don't have to do anything too laborious the following day. The next morning, brush then gargle with killer mouthwash. You're ready.

For the Quick-Fix Woman

Keep some mint chewing gum by the bed – and before you pounce, chew on a strip until your mouth no longer feels furry, then spit it out and stick it somewhere discreet.

For Him

He won't want to disrupt the moment by saying 'oh excuse me, let me nip to the bathroom to clean my teeth', but you won't particularly want to snog a man whose mouth tastes like death. So as part of your pounce-preparations, make him a cup of tea and stick it on his bedside table, so that just before kissing-point he can (aha!) take a bacteria-diluting swig. Or have a glass of Ribena handy. Or make him take a bite of an apple, for God's sake. Or avoid snogging him, and instead dispense little butterfly kisses all over his face.

Real Life Sex

Charlotte, 30: 'I did this to my husband about 4am. I couldn't sleep for some reason. He looked gorgeous lying there asleep, and I felt this sudden stab of desire, and thought "why waste him?!" The next day was Friday, so I figured he wouldn't be too furious at me for disturbing his beauty sleep. So I got under the covers and started giving him a blow-job. It certainly worked. He woke up with the biggest grin on his face! It made me feel incredibly sexy, and judging from his orgasm, I'm pretty certain he thought so too.'

Losing Control

Guess what won't have him begging for more? You holding your stomach in so hard your face turns purple. Of course, certain women do this because at some low point in their life a useless deadbeat saw fit to criticize their body – a classic is a porky boyfriend declaring confidently: you should do stomach exercises. Oh yes? And you should get yourself a blow-up doll because, unlike real women, they don't crease.

It's basic psychology that when people have a hang-up, they can't wait to foist it on someone else. So if he's whining about your stomach, it's because he's got a problem with his own. It's his problem – hand it back to him.

Most well-balanced men love women's tummies, and all their other soft curvy fleshy bits. What they don't like is a woman who cannot relax and enjoy sex because 'Ooh no, I look awful from that angle!' 'Eeek! No, it's embarrassing'! It bores them. Of course, they will manfully reassure you and mean it: 'Really, you look beautiful – I love your bottom.' But, even if he is patient, this constant need for praise becomes a drag.

Especially if you then throw it back in his face. When he says 'You're so sleek and beautiful, you remind me of an urban fox!' and you reply sulkily 'Well I feel like a scraggy old stoat!' you are being rude, not modest (an entirely overrated virtue anyhow).

Why? Because rejecting his compliment makes him feel foolish and, possibly – if you are an urban fox of the human race – annoyed with you for playing games. Do the elegant thing and accept the compliment. Any man worth a second glance doesn't give a damn that your stomach creases. The media created a big hoo-ha when Michael Hutchence abandoned Helena Christensen for Paula Yates – What! A man, leaving someone very pretty and very thin for someone quite pretty and quite thin and successful, funny, smart, witty, sexy, charismatic and clever? – The weirdo! Anyone with that attitude is mentally too young for sex.

Incentives to caring less:

- If you 'watch yourself' having sex with a critical eye, you won't relax, and he'll know it – your juices won't be flowing, and your muscles will be tense.
- Test your body, make it work for you – if you can make your body do a seven-mile hike, or an aerobics class, or a sky-dive, you've got to feel proud of it.
- Make the best of your body – creams, lotions, and potions, facials and massages – the more the merrier I say.
- Talk yourself up: no matter how ridiculous you feel, stand naked in front of the bathroom mirror and say ten

times 'I am a beautiful woman' – daily. Just lock the door first. The power of affirmation means you may start to believe. Don't snort. Do it.

The Worry Bunny

The woman who doesn't worry about whether he thinks her little toe isn't as aesthetically pleasing as it might be worries instead about whether, when her boss said 'Can you have that report finished by Tuesday' he was implying that she was a slow worker and thus planning to issue her with her P45 on the Wednesday. Maybe if she goes into the office on Sunday she can finish the report by Monday and maybe that will make her boss reconsider.

If thoughts like these creep into bed with you, there is no way you or he are going to have a ball of any description. If he can see your face, he'll be able to tell from your expression that you are not thinking about the deliciously naughty things he is attempting to do with you. If he can't, admittedly it's going to be harder, but the physical signs of preoccupation – aka non-arousal – will be there. You only get out of sex what you put in (so to speak). If your mind is elsewhere, your man is not going to have the time of his horizontal life.

Teach yourself to switch off after work – after 5.30pm, they're not paying you, so don't give them free brainpower. Furthermore, if there is a work problem (and don't convince yourself there's one purely because you like to worry), there's nothing you can do about it when your man is going down on you, so you may as well put the thought to one side.

To help yourself achieve this goal:

- Keep your bedroom free of anything to do with work.
- If something is truly bothering you, resolve that later today you will make a to-do list, and/or call a trusted colleague to discuss your anxieties. Now it should be easier to put your worries aside. And other distractions.
- Turn off the phone's ringer.
- Turn down the answer machine so that if your mother does ring while you are mid-passion to remind you to take the car in, her directions to the garage plus other gems of essential information (they wax it as well darling, for a really reasonable price, so ...), will not make you and your man deflate.
- Keep your surroundings tidy, because the faint whiff of cheese caused by long-mouldering coffee cups can easily put you off your stroke.
- And if there's something about him that puts you off your stroke – and it has been known for great lovers to have not quite the freshest breath in the world – one way to tackle it is to say 'I don't like kissing when my teeth feel scummy – I'd like to brush my teeth'. If he has a brain bigger than a Smartie, he'll think hmm, maybe I

should too, seeing as I haven't brushed mine since eating that onion burger two hours ago.

Subtle but firm ways to ensure he's super-clean:

- Teeth – 'I don't like kissing when my teeth feel scummy – let's brush our teeth before you transport me to the heights of ecstasy.'
- Groin – 'Let's have a bath first, I want to soap you down using my breasts'. (Don't make this an idle threat – make him stretch out in the bath, then lavishly lather up your torso, climb on top, and slip-slide up and down his pelvic region – you can finish off manually for that extra-squeaky effect).
- Hair – 'I'd like to give you a head massage,' (he'll probably think you mean his penis, but it will make him lunge for the bath). Again, hop in the bath, sit behind him, pour on a gloop of shampoo before he can object, then scrub for all you're worth in the name of massage. If you feel charitable let your hands wander southwards.

Baby Talk

Ugh. It's all very well in it's place – like, when you're two years old. But when you're a grown woman, who wants to drive her man wild with desire, it's inappropriate. Calling him Puppy or Wusskin occasionally, in privacy, when you want to persuade him to make you popcorn because you can't be bothered to arise from the sofa, is just about acceptable. Anything else is not.

If you want him to fancy you, keep your inner child inner. The last thing he wants to hear, when he's grinding away beneath you is – 'Ooh! Dat feels weeelly hard! Ooh, Chubblykins lubs dat wery much!' It makes him feel like he's a twelve year old committing an offence, and he may throw up. It transforms you from a powerful, sexy woman, into a silly little girl. The last thing you need.

Outercourse

Getting away from the idea that penetration is the goal of sex is difficult. After all, the survival of the species depends on it. Which means men and women are programmed to want it in an 'ooh really want it, please, let's do it, ahhh baby put it in NOW' kind of way – rather than faff and fiddle around for hours on end with other cute but less essential body parts. For the same evolutionary reason, the human body is programmed to hit on the easiest way (for it, personally) to achieve orgasm and then stick to that shortcut. This is great, if you want babies and only have 15 minutes to spare, less great if you prefer practising.

A quickie is fabulous, if you really should have set off for your boss's dinner party 20 minutes ago. But if you have two hours to spare, why waste 105 minutes of that watching quiz games? To make sex last longer, and become more fulfilling, you and he need to redefine it. Rather than seeing it as a horizontal line with 'kiss' at the beginning, 'grope' halfway through, and 'poke' at the end, try to see it as a circle. You begin at the centre, and can go in any direction, return to the centre, go off at a different tangent – there is no fixed goal.

If actual penetration is not the point, it forces you to try other things. This is great for the man because he isn't weighed down by performance anxiety. (And if your man has never ever been bothered by this, he's a liar and you'd be well advised to find out what else he's fibbing about). All men worry about their performance at some point. Outercourse gives you both the freedom to explore each other's bodies, perfect your manual and oral skills, experiment with sex toys, role play, to attempt to break the world record for the longest kiss (it's something like 17 days, so you'd better get comfortable) – anything you please. It forces you to be creative, and, when you do decide to go all the way – it's something pretty damn special.

Never be Fazed

Meaning, should you fart, it's not the end of the world and (more relevently) the relationship. Anyhow, he's more likely to fart than you are as, apparently men pass wind 12.7 times a day – compared to women who manage a modest 7.1. But, as luck would have it, you can bet that .1 pops out as he is wrestling off your knickers with his teeth. Don't let it cramp your style. The wisest procedure is to say something breezy (heheh!) such as sorry! I'll lay off the beans next time! or simply sorry! giggle briefly, then shut up about it. Don't make it a bigger deal than it is or he will start thinking of you as 'The Farter.'

What to do when the worst happens:

- You fanny fart: say, 'Wow! Sex to a fanfare'!
- He farts: say, 'Does that mean you're enjoying it?'
- He falls asleep during: go to sleep yourself and don't mention it.
- You fall asleep during: say, 'It was so blissful, I started to dream.' (You insulted him, let's face it).
- You wet yourself:* say, 'The feeling was so wild I lost control.'

* Anything more serious than that – you're on your own.

Not Trying too Hard

An ironic recommendation, considering the point of this book, but when a woman is trying to be too brilliant, too available, too everything in bed, it's slightly frightening for a guy. He wants it, but he doesn't want it. The raunchy man, the sensual man may understand, because he's tuned in to sensuality for sensuality's sake. But traditionally, the average man – even if he is a toad to your princess – thinks that every woman who looks at him instead of through him wants to drag him up the aisle, spend all his money, change his eating habits, nag him to within an inch of his life, and never allow him out to the pub. As if!

Even so, excitable new flames and tad conservative men especially, are quick to mistake an enthusiastic perfectionist for a wannabe-wife. They never realize that most sensible women have no desperate wish to formally attach themselves to a partner who has about as much get up and go as a beige carpet, even if he does have a nice smile. They don't comprehend that single women are not all blindly searching for commitment with every man they go to bed with. Sure, we may fantasize about what our kids would look like, within minutes of meeting some guy with long eyelashes – but that's it.

In reality, most of us are fantastically picky. If only men knew how often women think you'll do – for now, they'd be far more relaxed about relationships – and uninhibited, extravagant, just-for-the-thrill-of-it sex.

Instead, if a woman thinks 'tonight, I want some fun' and lays out the proverbial red carpet, possibly does herself up in an itchy garter belt, makes a nice dinner (he's not to know the M&S packets are at the bottom of the bin), lights some candles, pours some wine, plays footsie with him under the table, and maybe lets her foot wander north – the ungrateful sod is prone to think 'Uh-oh, she wants to marry me!' and sex suffers because he's on edge.

When all she really really wants is to flirt, enjoy herself, roger him senseless, and make him dizzy with longing – because that is fun. Acquiring a mother-in-law is not. Make it plain you're not after a mother-in-law (even if you are) and he will be more amenable to being driven crazy in bed – and begging for more.

How to not try too hard (in his eyes):

- Hide this book.
- Say – in response to any hint from him that he thinks you're over-keen – 'You think I want to marry you, don't you?! Darling, I want to have fun, I don't want to be a wife.' (Say this in jolly tone, but say 'wife' with a sneer. Now you've squashed his cocky speculation flat).
- Or 'I thought I'd make a fuss tonight. But don't get used to it.'

- Talk about how you're planning something (a holiday, a round-the-world trip), and make it clear you're not inviting him.
- If you don't feel like sex one time, don't have it.

Don't Use Sex as a Reassurance Tool

Some women regard sex as an emotional manipulator – a way to make him lurrrrrve you. This is bad. Certainly, if the love is already there, sex can bump it along a bit. And it is the best way of bonding, reaffirming intimacy, showing you adore each other, reminding yourselves how much pleasure you get from your relationship together, if you have a relationship together. This is why, once you prod your lazy long-term man into switching off the telly and switching onto your G-spot, he becomes a whole lot more cheerful, and you stop squabbling for a while.

But, especially at the beginning of a relationship, no matter how much of an excitable new flame he is, sex is never a guarantee that he loves you. It can prompt lust, awe, infatuation (all good, respectable feelings), but rarely love. And in their hearts, women know this. Which is why wheedling a lukewarm man into having sex with her – even if it is great – often makes a woman feel empty-ish inside. She feels as if she's begged, when he is the one who should be begging! (Or that's how he should see it). If he feels you want sex from him in a needy way (rather than a purely, physically greedy way), he'll get nervous. A healthy sexual appetite is fine. But no one feels great about a sympathy-fuck.

But – there is an up-side to this. If he doesn't want to have sex one day when you do, it doesn't mean he doesn't love you. If, one bright Sunday morning, you don't have much planned and yet he shows no inclination for sex and any overtures you make in that direction are ignored, don't interpret it as anything sinister. It does not mean he doesn't fancy you anymore. Don't declare dramatically, 'You make me feel like a tarantula!' or words to that effect. Some days, he just doesn't feel like sex, full stop, no hidden meaning.

If you make him feel guilty about not having sex, he'll start to feel sex with you is an obligation. Horror! Whereas if you have a healthy 'We didn't have sex today and so what, we'll probably have it sometime very soon, and further-more, he is as much in lust with me as he was yesterday' attitude, he will regard sex with you as a pleasure. As one man explained to his woman on refusing sex (they'd already done it twice that day), 'Sex with you is wonderful. But it's like eating a whole chocolate cake. I can't do it every day, three times a day. It's too much.'

He's having a celibate day so:

- go shopping
- read a good book

- stay in bed (sleeping)
- do something indulgent together – knickerbocker glory sharing? Day trip to Paris? Drive to the coast for fish 'n' chips?
- DIY (the sex, not the house).

Remember He's Trying to Impress You Too

And his body can let him down far more obviously than yours. When the worst happens – think forcing a marshmallow through a keyhole – it is intensely depressing. No, not for you – for him. You may be annoyed, frustrated, and offended (how dare he not get an erection? How dare it go down? Waste of my time! All mouth, no trouser! What's wrong with him? What's wrong with me?), but he feels a whole lot worse. Failing to get it up hacks at the very core of the male sexual ego. Tread very carefully. How you behave is crucial to his future performance.

Real Life Sex (or how not to do it)

Brian, 32: 'It was my first night with a woman I'd chased for months. We'd had a long flirtation, but when it came to the crunch, I was petrified with shyness. In my head I was up for it. But the feelings just wouldn't translate to er, lower down. It could have been okay, had she been understanding. But she was crushing. I think she took it personally. She raised an eyebrow, nodded towards my groin, and said "happens often, does it?" I wanted to crawl away. I felt a failure as a man. I could never expose myself – literally and figuratively – to someone that cruel again.

If sex is a flop, do:

- Say 'Let's just kiss.'
- Act lovingly, patiently but not condescendingly.
- Say 'We can do other things,' for example...
- Remind yourself that sex is not going to be mind-blowing every time, no matter how in lust you are.
- Pretend it doesn't matter and distract him. The best way to make sure Mr Softy doesn't reoccur is to shrug it off. If he shrugs it off, he looks uncaring. So you shrug it off.
- Resolve that next time you plan some hot action, he should restrict himself to one pint, not ten.
- If he apologises, say it doesn't matter or something similar. This is no time to tell the truth.

If sex is a flop, don't:

- Say 'Is it me?' (pathetic, whiny, irritating).
- Say 'What's wrong with you?' (rude, blunt, cruel, aggressive).
- Tut or huff or cry (impatient, rude, blunt, cruel, selfish).
- Show any other negative emotion (not only will he resent you, next time – if there is a next time – he's more likely to be tense, nervous, anxious and flaccid).

- Say 'Maybe if you didn't drink so much you might be able to perform,' (sarcastic, and all of the above).

Are you the Mistress of Mischief?

You should be. To reiterate the main point: sex should be fun. So be cheeky. Most human beings have a terror of being boring (which is why boring people so often insist 'oh I'm mad, me!'). Consequently, whatever the truth may be, many men like to think of themselves as having a wild n' crazy sex life. This is where you come in. Don't feel afraid to act on instinct, be playful, silly occasionally, surprise him, if it feels right – do it, make him laugh during sex (not at you) he'll think of himself as having a wild sex life. Because in his head, brilliant and wild are interchangeable.

Which means (happily) wild to the average man doesn't mean making love while dangling from a suspension bridge. It means doing something he hasn't done before. So, give him a blow job when he's on the phone to his mother (if he bats away your hands too furiously, you may have to adjust to his idea of wild). Pounce on him in the middle of the night, two nights running. Do it on the sofa before his flatmate gets home (then scramble to grab your clothes as the key turns in the lock). Don't wear any knickers – to the pub, or somewhere posh. Find somewhere remote, outdoors, and do it there. He'll feel lusty, highly-sexed, and vastly superior to all the men he knows.

Wild means different things to different men (feel free to mix 'n' match).

- To the tad conservative man, it's anything with handcuffs.
- To the excitable new flame, it's yanking down the essentials and doing it in a doorway after a great night out because you just can't wait to get home
- To the raunchy man, it's videoing you masturbating yourself to wild orgasm, somewhere you shouldn't be, and him joining in.
- To the lazy long-term man, it's doing it during the week.
- To the romantic man, it's making a champagne picnic and doing it outdoors, somewhere pretty.

Mood Judging

When we are in lust we are often blind to the obvious.
(The human race might die out otherwise). Anyhow – the
obvious fact is, that he – like you – is not always going to
feel like the same sort of sex. It's easy to get stuck into the
idea that loverboy likes to do it sweatily, standing up in
the hallway – or loudly, in the garden, and then launch
into that type of lovemaking, to perform to perceived
expectations. This isn't what will have him on his knees.
He desires a woman who understands what he wants
(excruciatingly difficult as this is) and some days, when
he's feeling sharp, he'll want to have wild flingy-about sex,
and other days, when his team has been relegated, he'll
want to have comfortable, cosy, cuddly sex. You're not
having sex with a man, you're having sex with him.

If He's Tired, Drop It

The most dispiriting eventuality for a woman is when her man falls asleep on the job. Men are like dogs – they can doze off anywhere. It is just about unbelievable when it happens. You think 'hang on – I am here, naked. I am offering myself for your delectation. We are in the middle of lovemaking. And you've dropped off! Yet you manage to stay awake through Brookside!' You better believe it. Don't take it personally (although, in the circumstances, that's a tall order). He's probably had too much to drink/too many late nights/too much excitement.

Don't try to shake him awake and act indignant. There's no point. It's highly embarrassing for him and for you, even though the obvious reason is that he's tired, drunk, or both. It's hardly likely that sex with you is so soporific he couldn't keep awake, so why add guilt to an already unsexy concoction? It's more likely that even though he was exhausted, he really truly wanted to have sex with you but the excitement overcame him. Just give in gracefully, kick or pinch him if he starts snoring, and do something dignified like have a bubble bath or watch *Fawlty Towers* videos.

What to do when he drops off during:

- Roll off him and resolve to tease him in the morning.
- Resolve that next time you feel sleepy when he's going down on you, you won't feel bad about a brief doze.
- Grab a book, pretend to be absorbed, then pinch him hard, and – when he leaps awake – pretend innocence.

What not to do:

- Roll off him and resolve to tease him in the morning, afternoon, evening, the following morning.
- Sulk.
- Shake him awake and force him to continue.

Be Greedy

Traditionally, little girls are conditioned against greediness. Hence, silly old-fashioned notions such as eating like a bird, or being patient linger in some women's heads as desirable traits. Other people often apply that guilt-laden term 'greed' when they see you going after what you want – you're greedy for love/status/money – because envious, mean-spirited people know they have a good chance of inducing self-doubt in a woman if they call her greedy. In fact, all this greediness means is that she wants those things. And why not?

Similarly, being 'greedy' about sex is something that many women shrink from. Some foolish men use terms like 'insatiable' 'demanding' or 'nymphomaniac' with a sneer. Why? Because they think it's er, unladylike. As this isn't a valid reason, we can conclude that it is fine and dandy for a woman to want whatever she wants in sex. And, if she isn't getting it, to demand it. Now! And again!

If a man is worth getting into bed for, he'll be delighted to give it to you, as often as he has the strength to. The best men are hugely turned on by women who aren't scared of needing, who demand an equal share of the pie – in the bedroom and at the dinner table.

Three delicious reasons to be sexually greedy:

- If you tell him what you want, he's more inclined to tell you what he wants – it's the best way to get in perfect sexy synch.
- Or just do it – when you take control it's arousing for him.
- If you don't take risks you reduce your chances of being rejected but also miss out on potential pleasure. What happened to the girl who did nothing? Nothing.

The Inconvenience!

Plan not to plan. It is hard to feel frenzied, sensual, melty, delirious, lustful, and abandoned when you know you have to be at Asda in 45 minutes. If you have ever uttered the words, 'Let's have sex, say, in about 15 minutes darling, then at about 11 we can go shopping', go directly to the sink and rinse your mouth out. Being so clinical and organised and Mary Poppins about sex is the antithesis of passion. It's as if you regard sex as yet one more chore to squeeze in after you've washed up the breakfast things and before you visit your parents. He'll feel as sexy as an old turnip because he thinks (rightly) that you expect him to perform to order.

Well, of course you do, but rapping out a start-time and deadline makes that unfetchingly obvious. If you want to have sex with him after you've washed up the break-fast things, start being touchy-feely and affectionate the minute you both wake up. The romantic man, the tad con-servative man, even the raunchy man – make that all men – often find it as difficult as women to snap into a sultry mood without warning. Whereas if you start laying the groundwork a few hours before, by the time the breakfast things have been cleared (or at least shoved to one side) he'll be feeling frisky without you having to say a word.

'It just happened'

- Make him late. Grab him when you are about to have guests round for dinner. Either a quickie, or, if they're easygoing friends, ring and say, 'We're running late with the food – can you make it 8.30 not 8.00?'
- Don't say 'Darling, tonight I think we should have sex.' It's too pressurizing. Say 'Let's have an evening to ourselves – we'll order in something and watch a video.' Then, once you're cosied up on the sofa, start smooching, and see what happens.
- Resolve to see sex as a priority.* That means doing it before dinner, before you ring your friends, before you water the plants.

---

* You may laugh, two weeks into a relationship, but two years later, you won't!

Loud and Proud

First off — you don't have to say anything, much. You just have to make an appreciative noise. Silent lovemaking can be wonderful — after all, sex is supposed to be the international language — but making a noise is so expressive. It flatters his ego and spurs him on to greater things. Cunnilingus was once described by some uninspired guy as dark and lonely work — either because his woman was rolling her eyes in pleasure, grimacing with joy, and had swallowed her tongue, or (and this is the better bet, considering his sourness) had fallen asleep.

If she had roused herself to commentate — for example: 'Oooh! Oh yes! Oh my god! Oh no! Yow! Shriek! Oh more!!' etc., he might not have felt so abandoned. He might have had some inkling of how she felt, if she liked it, and what pressure and stroke she preferred. Short of shining a torch down there, she couldn't have helped with the darkness, but she could have alleviated the loneliness. (Although he does sound like a miserable grump who wasn't capable of pausing for a second and demanding feedback).

Making a rumpus is a way of letting the other party know you are enjoying yourself, rather like the way people are more likely to laugh out loud at something funny when their friends are present. Even better, exaggerating your enthusiasm actually makes a concrete difference to how you feel physically. It certainly makes a difference to how he feels physically. Admittedly, the tad conservative man might be a little scared (he's wondering, are you in pain?). But the raunchy man, the excitable new flame, the romantic man, and even the rather surprised but pleasantly so lazy long-term man will appreciate your gusto. He takes it as a compliment to him. Which makes his head swell (and other bits).

Making Yourself Heard

Michelle, 25, says 'I admit — I am a screamer! Only one guy ever had a problem. He said he couldn't concentrate. But my current boyfriend loves it. He says it makes him hot because it is so obvious how much I'm loving it. I am louder than I need to be, but shouting seems to amplify the sensations too. And it's fun! Anyhow, my boyfriend is not exactly a mouse himself — our neighbours must hate us.'

Knicker Tricks One

Isn't sleaziness what makes sex so attractive? Lower your principles. Do something tacky. When you're sitting in a restaurant, go to the ladies, remove your knickers, then scrunch them up in your hand and sweetly pass them to your man. Or do it at the table. Someone did this in a film – can't recall who – but I bet her knickers weren't crotchless. Crotchless knickers might be a cliché but who gives a stuff? If your sexual image is elegant candlelight, white sheets, gossamer lingerie and perfect hair, your man is probably gagging for a bit of grubbiness.

Knicker Tricks Two

Or, as he plops himself down on the kitchen chair for a cup of tea, sit on his lap, wriggle around, unzip his trousers, tease him to red alert, pull your knickers to one side, bend over the table, and let him 'take you.' Oh the urgency! He'll love it. (This pulling of knickers to one side in order to gain rapid access is immensely arousing to men – even though the side of the gusset may chafe his manhood. If you think he's the sensitive type, just hold your knickers aside while he marvels at how unbelievably lucky he is).

The Real Cardinal Sin: Faking Orgasms

It's the saddest thing you can do. It's weedy, it's the easy option, it's a waste. It's patronising to him, and to yourself. It makes the whole experience a sham. Maybe you've faked ever since you told him once that you didn't orgasm and he acted as if it was your fault. If so, he's either inexperienced or as sensitive as a tree stump and about as thick. He may be a man who's struck lucky and only fallen into bed with women who orgasm easily. The upshot? He thinks he's Mr Darcy. Then he meets a woman — you — who requires a little finesse and is as stumped as the England cricket team.

So he prefers to ignore the problem. You're helping him. You think you're making sex better for him (at your expense), but you're not. Anyhow, the point here is you, not him. This does not contradict this book's title — if you don't count your own pleasure as equal to his, then you may give him a fun flutter between the sheets, but soon enough he'll sense that something is lacking. Guess what it is? We could be poetic and say it's your soul. More relevantly, it's your sexuality. By denying yourself fulfilment, you deny it. You're going through the motions. Your communication level is zero. How can that be great sex?

Unless you take your own pleasure as seriously as you take his, your sex life with him will always be limited. And, incidentally, the sex will be more satisfying for him if you really do climax. He will feel your pleasure – he will witness you experience the raw, primeval joy of a deep, warm, rippling, shivery, right-down-to-the-toes pink-cheeked orgasm. No amount of hammy thrashing can reproduce that feeling. When a woman's orgasm builds, she and her partner can often both feel it coming. When you climax from penetration, your vaginal muscles spasm and grip his penis – it is superlative.

How to Make it Better

That said, many women don't feel able to climax from penetration. Thankfully, it isn't GCSE maths, so it isn't obligatory. A climax from oral sex will do just as nicely. But let's start from the absolute basics. Let's presume you haven't had an orgasm ever. The five steps to achieving one are:

- Learning to masturbate. If you don't know how to please yourself, it's hypocritical to expect him to. Grab a mirror, lock the bathroom door, strip, open your legs. Acquaint yourself with your vagina. Your clitoris. Touch, explore. Use your hand or a vibrator. Find out what makes you feel good. If you feel unaroused, maybe read some erotica while prodding, rubbing, stroking.
- Once you can make yourself orgasm, you are equipped to show him how to please you. Even if it's unspoken knowledge between you that you haven't had an orgasm, you don't have to say anything as ghastly as Er, I've been faking so far, and today I want you to give me a real orgasm. If it's too eeksome, you don't have to say a word. Just show him. When you're writhing naked together, take his hand and place it where you want it

to be. Show him the pressure, and the stroke. Breathe slowly and deeply to relax yourself.

- Unless he's mad, he is not going to say 'Er, what are you doing?' He's going to think 'wow'! If you think it seems rather silent and purposeful, just murmer 'that feels good' or 'it feels great when you do that'. Reward him for good behaviour and he'll repeat it. Feel free to bestow sexual favours.

- Another tack – (and if your excitable new flame, raunchy man, romantic man and, yes, your tad conservative man is worth holding on to he's going to be keen to please), – is to play the following game: he goes down on you, and you give him marks out of ten for intensity. You are NOT testing his prowess. You are finding out together what feels good for you. Make sure he's well rested. He could be down there for hours. Your mission is to relax and enjoy it. If you get tense you will find it nearly impossible to climax. Don't do this twenty minutes before you're due at your great aunt's birthday bash.

- Practice makes perfect. If your man is any man at all, he's going to enjoy finding out what does it for you. It may take weeks or months (shame!), but when you finally get there, the kick – let alone the orgasm itself – is indescribable. He's made you feel good, he's watched you bloom – guess how good he feels about himself, about sex with you now?

- If you can orgasm from oral sex then the potential is there to orgasm from penetration. A good position to increase your chances is you on top. Lean forward or back, tell him 'slower' or 'faster' – and believe it can happen. Don't get tense if it doesn't, and when you're least expecting it – it may surprise you.

Never Generalize

There are many generalisations made about men – they can orgasm at the drop of a knicker. They think foreplay is a waste of minutes. They like to take control in bed. Any of those may be true of some men, aged 17 and a half (and some men who have never aged mentally beyond their teens). But the majority grow out of it. Most well-adjusted men cannot produce a boner in 20 seconds flat just because you said 'Let's do it! Now!' They like affection and to be touched, caressed and kissed and aroused same as most women do. And they hate to feel that they are expected to do all the work.

Note
just because your last boyfriend loved it when you scraped your nails down his back, doesn't mean this boyfriend will.

Nine Ways To Make Him Feel Top
- Ask him what turns him on.
- Never assume he knows what turns you on (and vice versa). Why should he? Help him out.

- Ask him if he has a fantasy he hasn't tried (and know how to say 'not on your life, sweetheart' in a kindly way).
- Caress his whole body and take 40 minutes about it.
- Initiate sex, don't always wait for him to.
- Initiate sex in a seductive way – not a blunt way (although the phrase 'fancy a shag?' is cute in the right context).
- But don't assume that every cuddle should lead to full sex.
- Don't strop if he doesn't get an erection the minute you touch him.
- Don't turn down his advances more than three times in a row.

Quick One

But do turn him down if you are resolutely not in the mood. Some men excel at the art of persuasion. If you do not want to be persuaded because, at this particular moment, the idea of friction with another human being makes you recoil, just say no.

Actually, don't just say 'No!' Because 'No!' – said narkily and accompanied by a smart snapping together of legs – can be hurtful to a man. Say, 'No!' in, um, a loving, non-rejecting type way. Maybe kiss him? Look into his eyes and say 'I don't feel that hot today, but save your energy for tomorrow' but please, don't say 'Yes.'

If you say 'yes' when you mean 'leave me alone', unless you are a superb actress, your half-heartedness will become embarrassingly apparent mid-bonk. This will effect the opposite of making him beg you for more. No man – unless he is a real rat – likes to think you are humouring him. His sexual ego is severely dented, he blames you, and will either:

a get over it, or

b   emotionally and physically withdraw to salvage his self-esteem and punish you for hurting him, or

c   stomp off and find a woman who is willing to puff up his ego.

Of course, if he is a well-balanced individual, he will choose option a). But why not just say 'No!' in a sweet, nurturing, friendly way, promise him compensation, then curl up with a hot chocolate?

Novelty Value

Men are notorious for getting bored fast. Cue, an affair. Their risible excuse — when found out — is, they're genetically programmed to sow their oats in as many fields as possible. Or, it just happened. The truth is, if one partner — male or female — is unfaithful, it never just happens. There is something amiss with the relationship. Yet, whatever the specifics of the problem, many men blame their infidelity on that wildly imprecise state of mind: boredom.

There are no guarantees that your man (or indeed you) will stay in lust and/or in love forever. If there were, Interflora would go out of business. But to give your relationship the greatest chance of success, the smartest thing you can do is keep boredom (his and yours) at bay. Common traits of happy relationships include trust, friendship, respect, passion, laughter, fun and novelty.

If you want to keep him hopping around you, novelty is important. Novelty in your sex life isn't usually an issue with the excitable new flame, the raunchy man, the sensuous man — but other types are usually too slovenly or easy-going to protest. That doesn't mean they're content.

Men tend to be unwilling to discuss a problem until they reach breaking point. No need to let it get that far.

Keep doing what you did to attract him in the first place, keep enjoying yourselves together, restrict slumping together in front of the TV for five hours at a stretch to once a week. (Thought I'd save the hardest task till last). And, keep novelty at the top of your relationship list. That might mean giving each other hand-jobs at 30,000 feet under cover of those blankets they dole out on planes, taking salsa lessons together (then practising naked, at home), rutting on the bedroom floor occasionally rather than on the bed, or forcing yourselves to indulge in at least 30 minutes foreplay instead of your usual 15.

Why call sparkling up your sex life 'working at your relationship' when it's such extraordinary, delicious, rumbustuous fun? Especially when your horizontal talents reduce your gorgeous man to a blob of dizzy, dopey, delirious desire – the job satisfaction is incomparable. Division of chores and being nice to each other's families – that's working at your relationship. But that's another book altogether.